Spring-clean those Maths skills with CGP!

Blow away the winter cobwebs with this CGP Daily Practice Book — it'll help pupils' Maths skills sparkle in the spring sunshine!

There's a page of brilliant Maths practice for every school day of the spring term, all covering vital skills from the Year 3 curriculum.

It's perfect for use in class or at home, with plenty of examples and splashes of colour to keep things interesting. Bring on spring!

What CGP is all about

Our sole aim here at CGP is to produce the highest quality books — carefully written, immaculately presented and dangerously close to being funny.

Then we work our socks off to get them out to you — at the cheapest possible prices.

Contents

☑ Use the tick boxes to help keep a record of which tests have been attempted.

Week 1
- ☑ Day 1 1
- ☑ Day 2 2
- ☑ Day 3 3
- ☑ Day 4 4
- ☑ Day 5 5

Week 2
- ☑ Day 1 6
- ☑ Day 2 7
- ☑ Day 3 8
- ☑ Day 4 9
- ☑ Day 5 10

Week 3
- ☑ Day 1 11
- ☑ Day 2 12
- ☑ Day 3 13
- ☑ Day 4 14
- ☑ Day 5 15

Week 4
- ☑ Day 1 16
- ☑ Day 2 17
- ☑ Day 3 18
- ☑ Day 4 19
- ☑ Day 5 20

Week 5
- ☑ Day 1 21
- ☑ Day 2 22
- ☑ Day 3 23
- ☑ Day 4 24
- ☑ Day 5 25

Week 6
- ☑ Day 1 26
- ☑ Day 2 27
- ☑ Day 3 28
- ☑ Day 4 29
- ☑ Day 5 30

Week 7
- ☑ Day 1 31
- ☑ Day 2 32
- ☑ Day 3 33
- ☑ Day 4 34
- ☑ Day 5 35

Week 8
- ☑ Day 1 36
- ☑ Day 2 37
- ☑ Day 3 38
- ☑ Day 4 39
- ☑ Day 5 40

Week 9

- [✓] Day 1 41
- [✓] Day 2 42
- [✓] Day 3 43
- [✓] Day 4 44
- [✓] Day 5 45

Week 10

- [✓] Day 1 46
- [✓] Day 2 47
- [✓] Day 3 48
- [✓] Day 4 49
- [✓] Day 5 50

Week 11

- [✓] Day 1 51
- [✓] Day 2 52
- [✓] Day 3 53
- [✓] Day 4 54
- [✓] Day 5 55

Week 12

- [✓] Day 1 56
- [✓] Day 2 57
- [✓] Day 3 58
- [✓] Day 4 59
- [✓] Day 5 60

Answers 61

Published by CGP

ISBN: 978 1 78908 650 8

Editors: Tom Carney, Rachel Craig-McFeely, Georgina Fairclough, Katie Fernandez, Joseph Shaw, Sarah Williams

With thanks to Claire Plowman and Emma Chambers for the proofreading.

With thanks to Lottie Edwards for the copyright research.

Clipart from Corel®

1 pence coin © iStock.com/coopder1
2 pence coin © iStock.com/peterspiro
5p coin © iStock.com/duncan1890
10 pence coin © iStock.com/john shepherd
20 pence coin © iStock.com/Jaap2
50 pence coin © iStock.com/duncan1890

Printed by Elanders Ltd, Newcastle upon Tyne.
Based on the classic CGP style created by Richard Parsons.

Text, design, layout and original illustrations © Coordination Group Publications Ltd. (CGP) 2020
All rights reserved.

Photocopying this book is not permitted, even if you have a CLA licence.
Extra copies are available from CGP with next day delivery • 0800 1712 712 • www.cgpbooks.co.uk

How to Use this Book

- This book contains 60 daily practice tests.

- We've split them into 12 sections — that's roughly one for each week of the Year 3 spring term.

- Each week is made up of 5 tests, so there's one for every school day of the term (Monday – Friday).

- Each test should take about 10 minutes to complete.

- The tests contain a mix of topics from Year 3 Maths. New Year 3 topics are gradually introduced as you go through the book.

- The tests increase in difficulty as you progress through the term.

- Each test looks something like this:

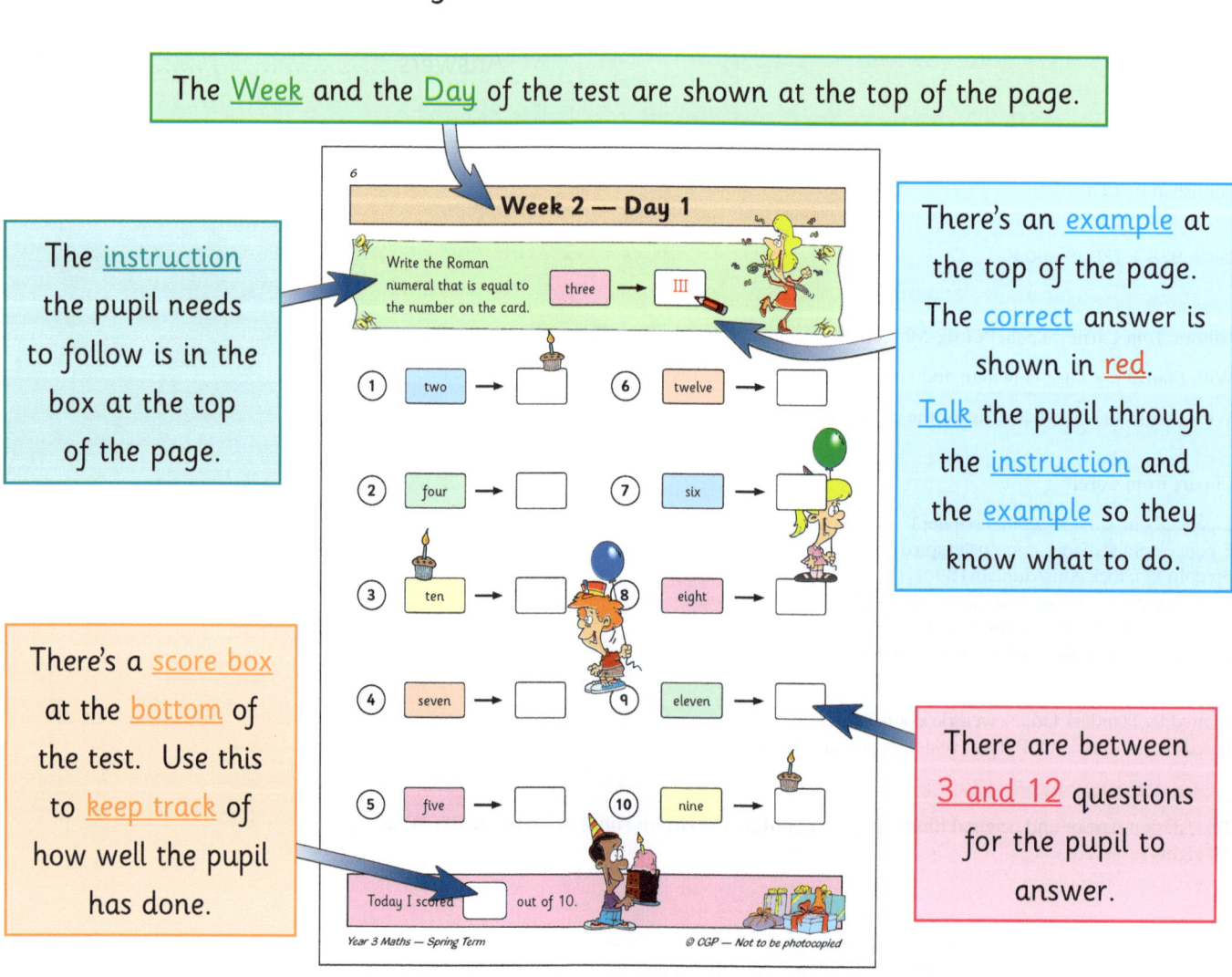

The Week and the Day of the test are shown at the top of the page.

The instruction the pupil needs to follow is in the box at the top of the page.

There's an example at the top of the page. The correct answer is shown in red. Talk the pupil through the instruction and the example so they know what to do.

There's a score box at the bottom of the test. Use this to keep track of how well the pupil has done.

There are between 3 and 12 questions for the pupil to answer.

Week 1 — Day 1

Fill in the missing numbers using your times tables.   9 × [2] = 18

1) 2 × ☐ = 24

7) 4 × ☐ = 28

2) 40 ÷ ☐ = 4

8) 16 ÷ ☐ = 8

3) 5 × ☐ = 30

9) 12 × ☐ = 36

4) 18 ÷ ☐ = 2

10) 32 ÷ ☐ = 8

5) 3 × ☐ = 33

11) 8 × ☐ = 24

6) 25 ÷ ☐ = 5

12) 48 ÷ ☐ = 12

Today I scored ☐ out of 12.

Week 1 — Day 2

Complete the tally chart by counting the hammers and nails.

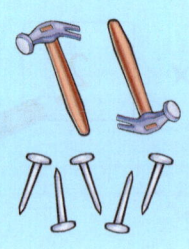

	Tally	Total
Hammers	| |	2
Nails	||||	5

1)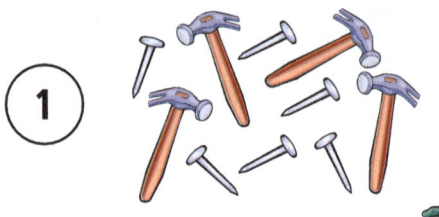

	Tally	Total
Hammers		
Nails		

2)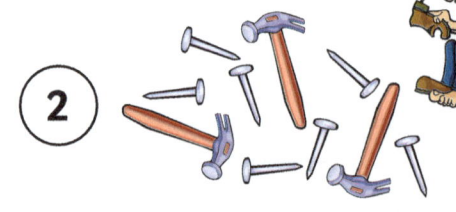

	Tally	Total
Hammers		
Nails		

3)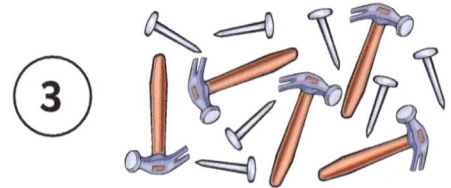

	Tally	Total
Hammers		
Nails		

4)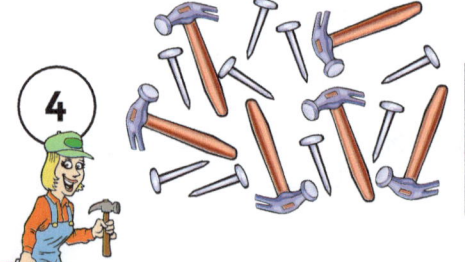

	Tally	Total
Hammers		
Nails		

5)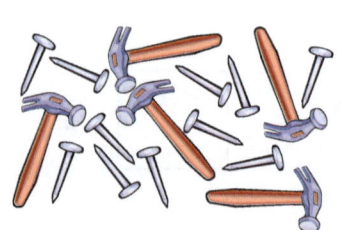

	Tally	Total
Hammers		
Nails		

Today I scored ☐ out of 5.

Year 3 Maths — Spring Term

Week 1 — Day 3

Write the number shown in words. | 178 | one hundred and seventy eight

1. 467
2. 346
3. 818
4. 621
5. 985
6. 799
7. 230
8. 504

Today I scored ▢ out of 8.

Week 1 — Day 4

Complete the calculation.

```
  2 7 8
+ 1 4 6
-------
  4 2 4
  1 1
```

1)
```
  1 3 5
+ 2 6 4
```

2)
```
  7 1 5
+ 1 8 3
```

3)
```
  4 6 2
+ 5 3 7
```

4)
```
  1 2 7
+ 2 4 3
```

5)
```
  2 2 9
+ 1 7 4
```

6)
```
  2 3 6
+ 5 7 6
```

7)
```
  3 5 7
+ 4 6 6
```

8)
```
  2 9 5
+ 1 3 7
```

9)
```
  1 8 6
+ 1 1 6
```

10)
```
  3 6 9
+ 1 4 7
```

Today I scored ☐ out of 10.

Year 3 Maths — Spring Term © CGP — Not to be photocopied

Week 1 — Day 5

Talia and Alika have the number of pineapples shown. They each give **half** of their pineapples to Manu. How many pineapples does Manu have?

Talia: 12, Alika: 16, Manu: 14

1) Talia 18, Alika 20, Manu ☐

2) Talia 46, Alika 16, Manu ☐

3) Talia 22, Alika 48, Manu ☐

4) Talia 26, Alika 40, Manu ☐

5) Talia 68, Alika 86, Manu ☐

6) Talia 70, Alika 36, Manu ☐

7) Talia 38, Alika 20, Manu ☐

8) Talia 54, Alika 44, Manu ☐

Today I scored ☐ out of 8.

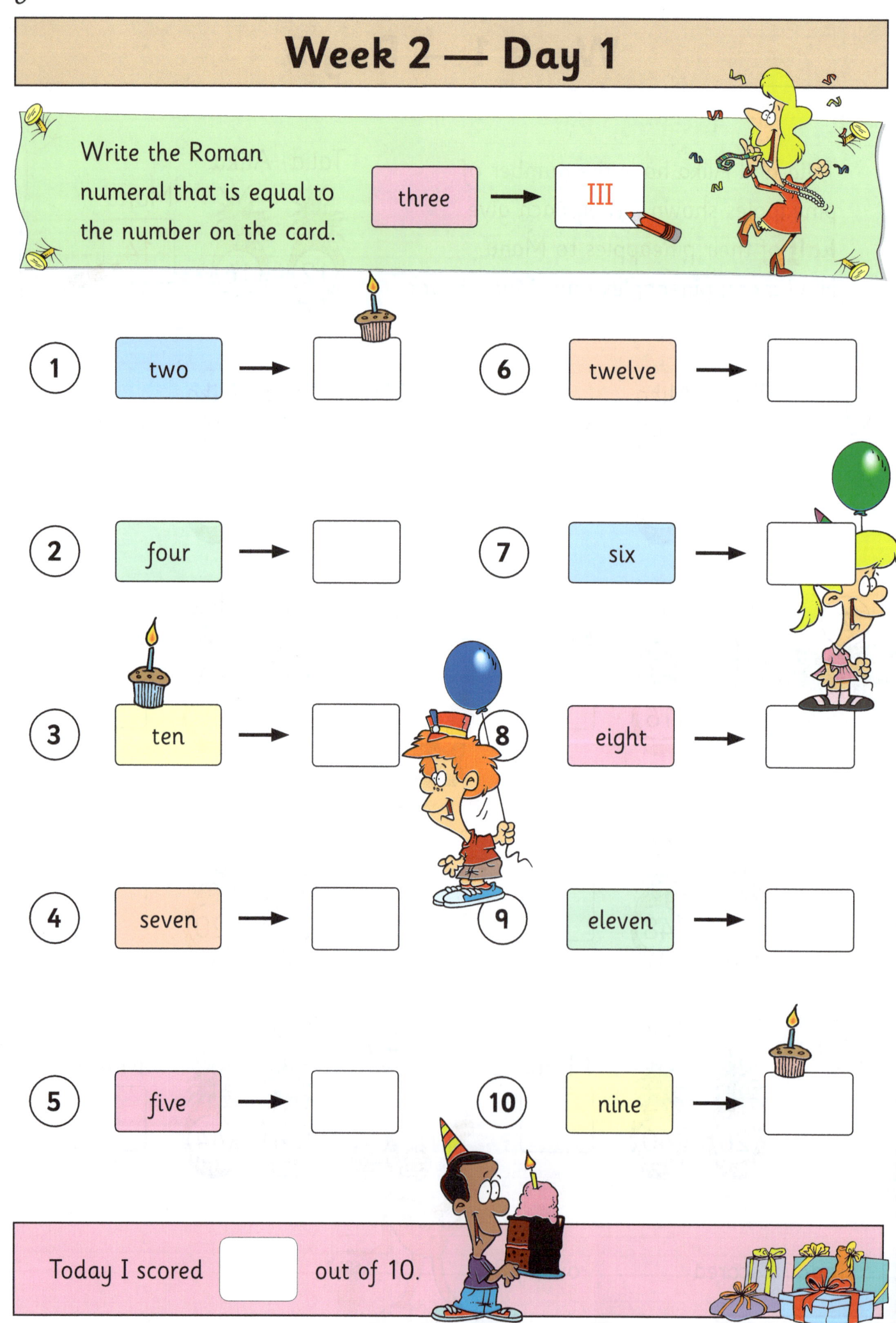

Week 2 — Day 2

Write < or > in the box.   19 > 12

1. 8 < 12
2. 15 < 51
3. 44 > 36
4. 87 < 92
5. 130 > 103
6. 148 > 139
7. 178 < 187
8. 201 < 211
9. 265 > 255
10. 273 > 237
11. 301 < 381
12. 387 > 378

Today I scored ☐ out of 12.

Week 2 — Day 3

Fill in the boxes to complete the sequence.   100   **200**   300   **400**

1) 300   ☐   500   600   ☐   800   900

2) ☐   ☐   200   300   400   500   600

3) 600   700   ☐   900   ☐   1100   1200

4) 700   600   500   ☐   300   200   ☐

5) ☐   1000   900   800   ☐   600   500

6) 600   ☐   400   300   200   100   ☐

Today I scored ☐ out of 6.

Week 2 — Day 4

Complete the calculation.

$$8\cancel{7}^{6}\cancel{4}^{1}$$
$$-125$$
$$\overline{749}$$

1)
```
  86
- 45
```

2)
```
 173
-  61
```

3)
```
 174
-143
```

4)
```
 225
-  75
```

5)
```
 360
-142
```

6)
```
 294
-238
```

7)
```
 312
-108
```

8)
```
 268
-249
```

9)
```
 362
-135
```

10)
```
 404
-211
```

Today I scored ☐ out of 10.

Week 2 — Day 5

Work out how many books each person read.

4 friends read 12 books one year and 16 books the next. They all read the same number of books.

7 books

1. 2 friends read 10 books one year and 14 books the next. They both read the same number of books.

   ☐ books

2. 4 friends read 15 books one year and 9 books the next. They all read the same number of books.

   ☐ books

3. 2 friends read 11 books one year and 7 books the next. They all read the same number of books.

   ☐ books

4. 10 friends read 27 books one year and 23 books the next. They all read the same number of books.

   ☐ books

5. 3 friends read 9 books one year and 18 books the next. They all read the same number of books.

   ☐ books

6. 5 friends read 24 books one year and 21 books the next. They all read the same number of books.

   ☐ books

Today I scored ☐ out of 6.

Week 3 — Day 1

Write down the number that each arrow points to.

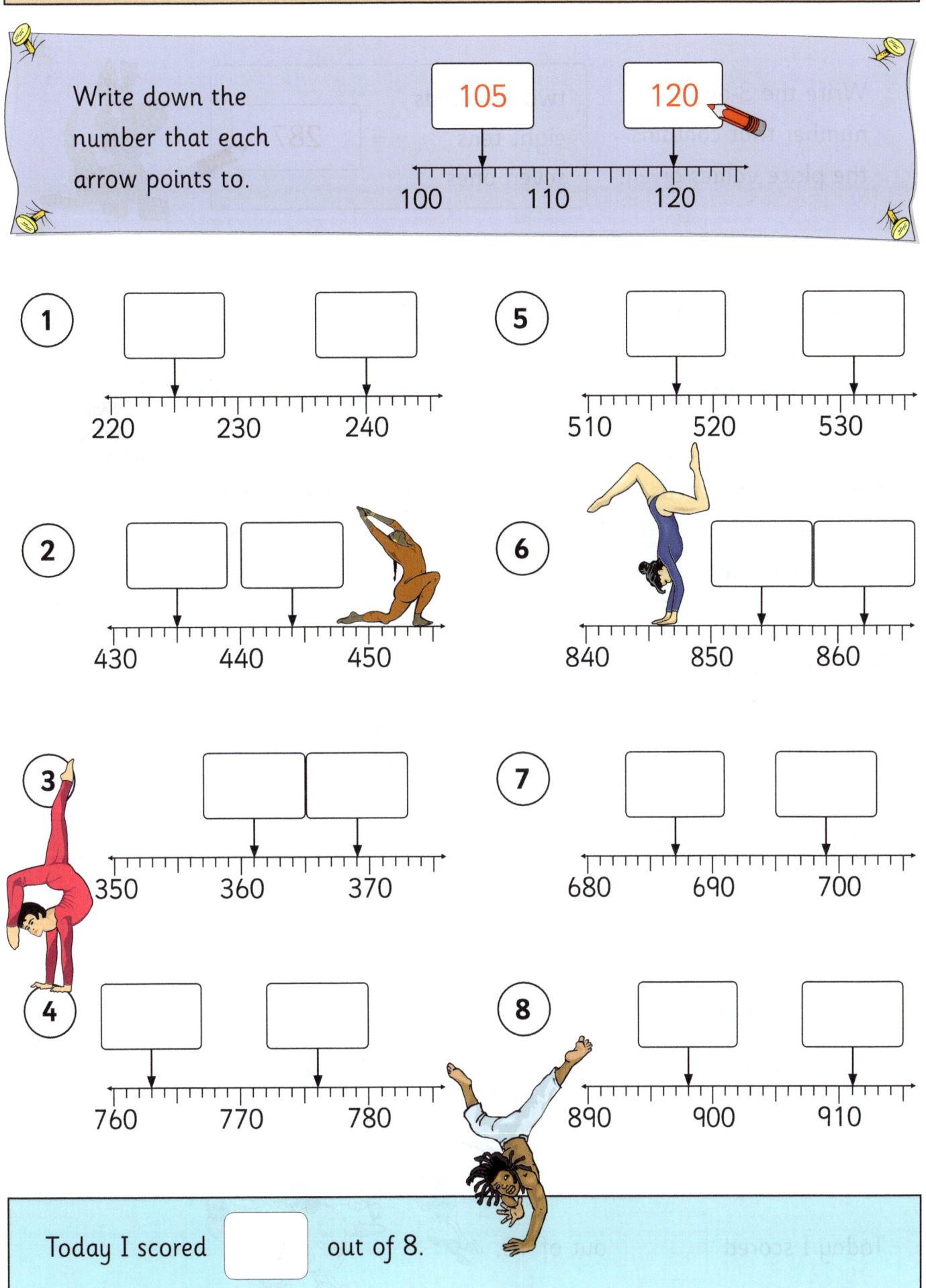

Today I scored ☐ out of 8.

Week 3 — Day 2

Write the 3-digit number that contains the place values given.

two hundreds
eight tens   = 287
seven ones

1) one hundred
   five tens   =
   three ones

2) three hundreds
   four tens   =
   nine ones

3) five hundreds
   zero tens   =
   six ones

4) four hundreds
   seven tens   =
   eight ones

5) six hundreds
   four tens   =
   three ones

6) one ten
   six ones   =
   eight hundreds

7) seven hundreds
   three ones   =
   five tens

8) zero ones
   two tens   =
   eight hundreds

9) zero hundreds
   six ones   =
   nine tens

10) three ones
    zero tens   =
    nine hundreds

Today I scored [ ] out of 10.

Year 3 Maths — Spring Term   © CGP — Not to be photocopied

Week 3 — Day 3

A horse eats the number of red and green apples shown. How many more red apples than green apples did it eat?

1) 36, 11, ☐
2) 29, 15, ☐
3) 47, 23, ☐
4) 23, 14, ☐
5) 61, 46, ☐
6) 56, 27, ☐
7) 57, 38, ☐
8) 75, 58, ☐
9) 103, 48, ☐
10) 196, 119, ☐

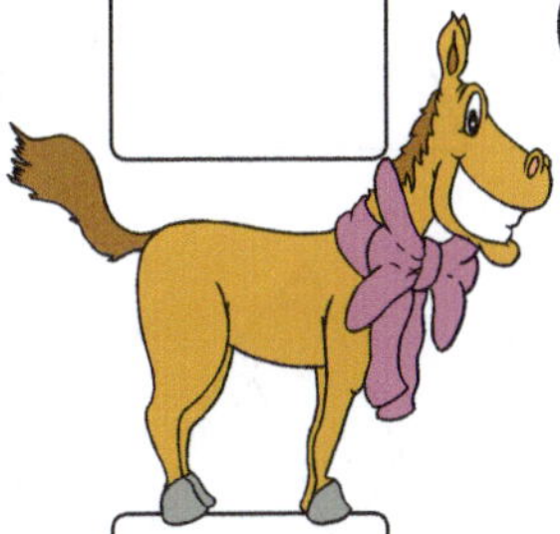

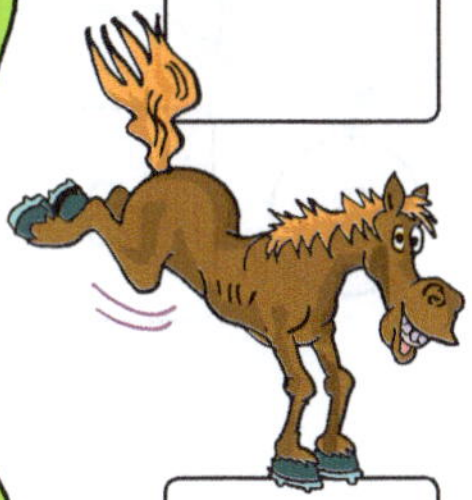

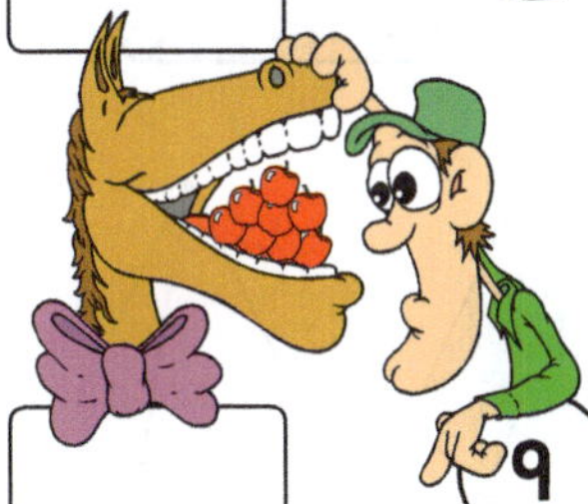

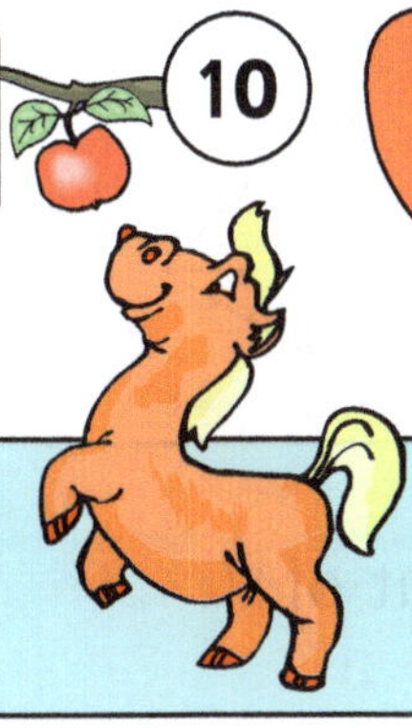

Today I scored ☐ out of 10.

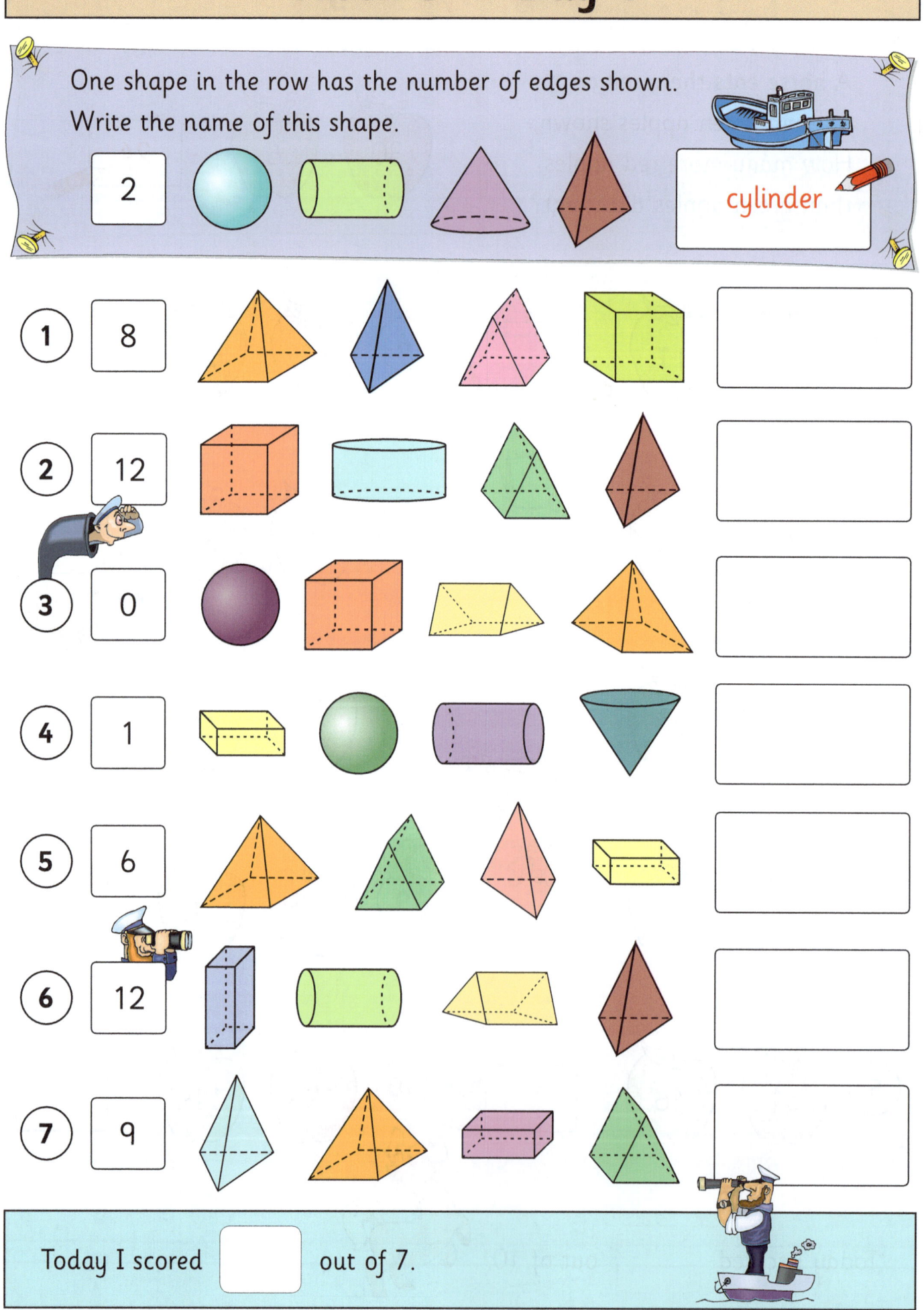

Week 3 — Day 5

Put the numbers on the coloured cards into the calculation to make the **biggest** answer you can.

| 1 | 2 | 3 | 4 |

4 2 + 3 1 = 73

1. 5 3 1 4   ☐☐ + ☐☐ = ☐
2. 1 1 6 2   ☐☐ + ☐☐ = ☐
3. 4 2 1 8   ☐☐ + ☐☐ = ☐
4. 6 5 2 7   ☐☐ + ☐☐ = ☐
5. 2 8 9 3   ☐☐ + ☐☐ = ☐
6. 5 3 7 5   ☐☐ + ☐☐ = ☐
7. 7 9 5 1   ☐☐ + ☐☐ = ☐
8. 7 9 8 5   ☐☐ + ☐☐ = ☐

Today I scored ☐ out of 8.

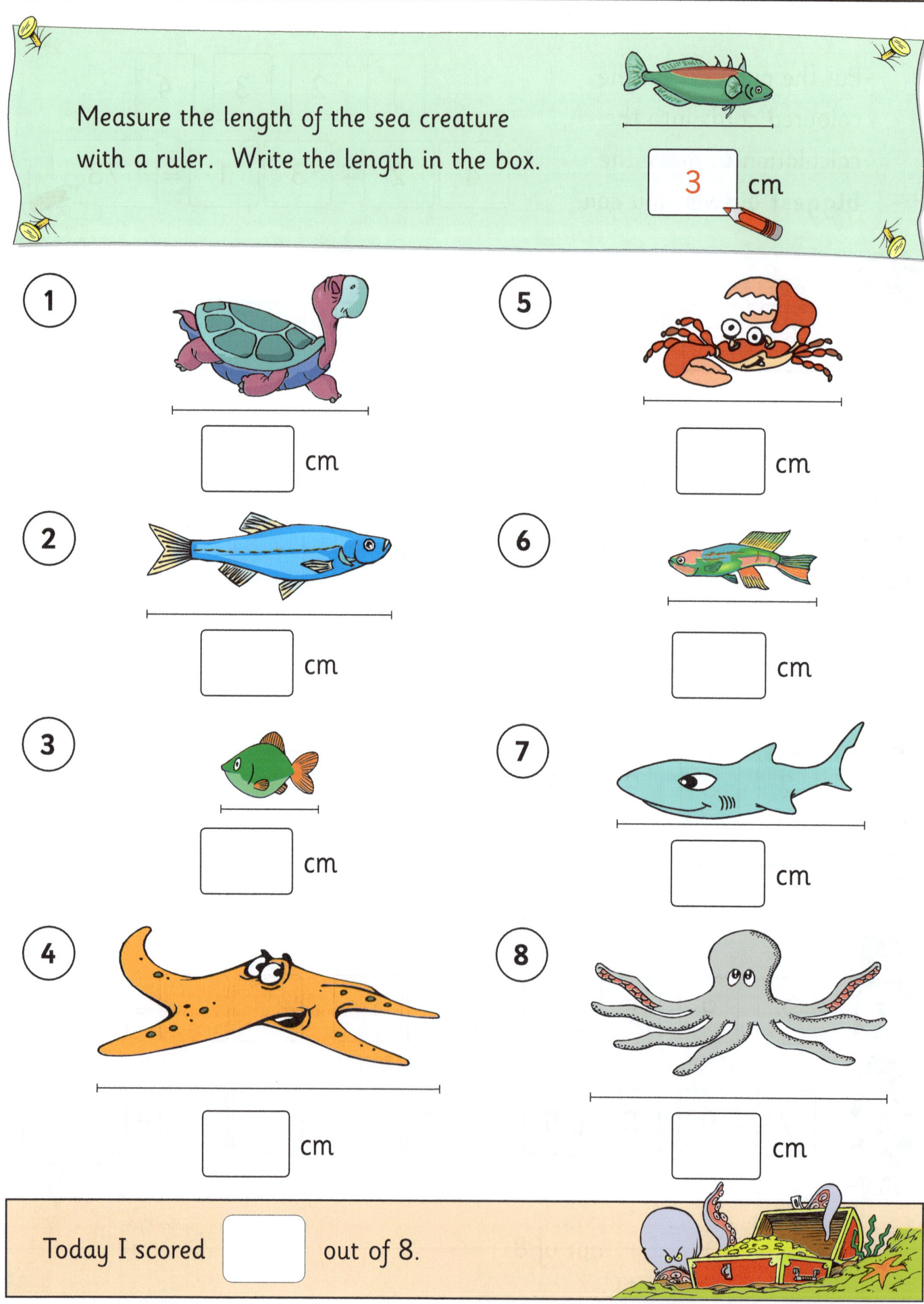

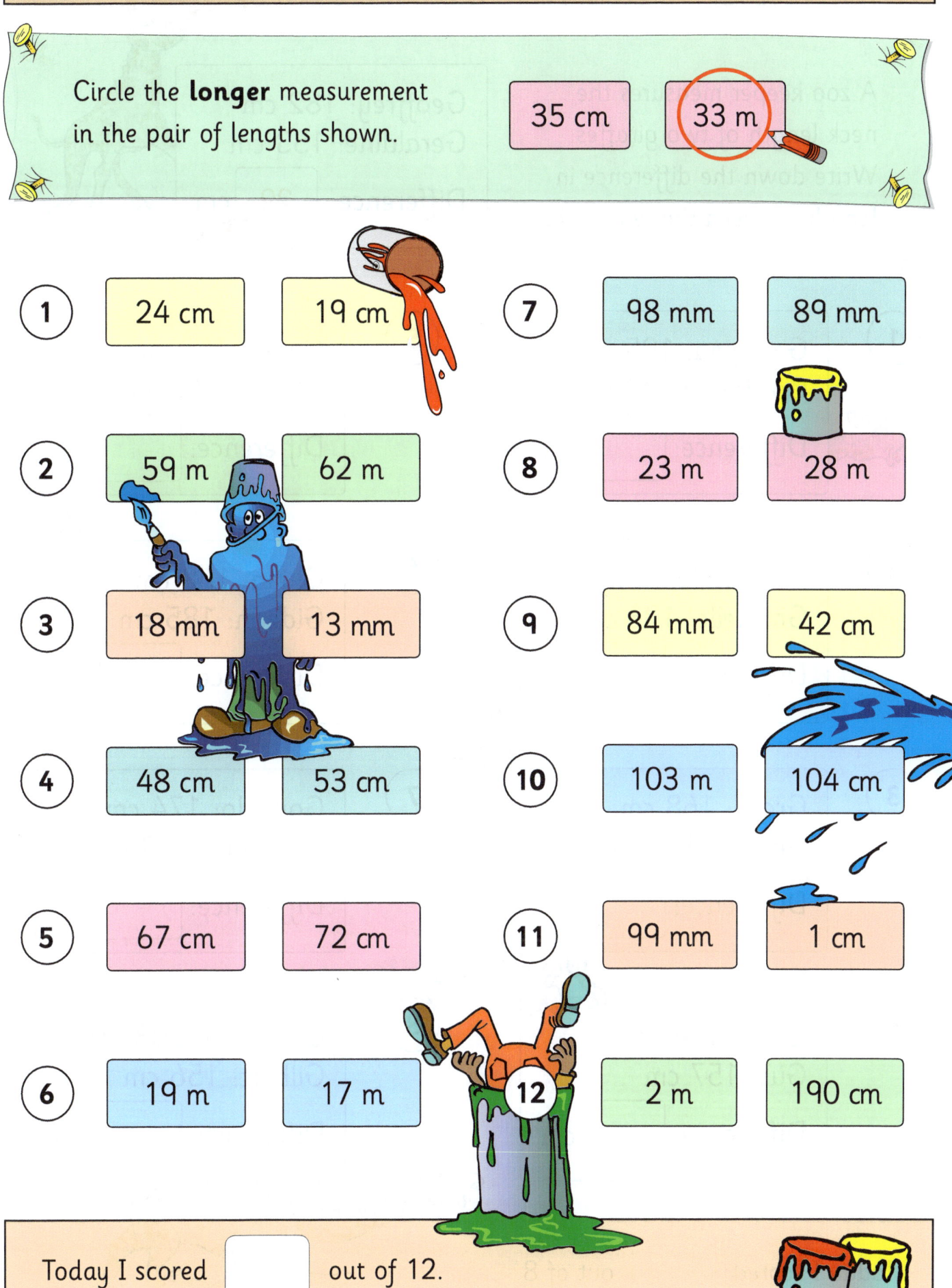

Week 4 — Day 3

A zoo keeper measures the neck length of two giraffes. Write down the difference in length between the two necks.

Geoffrey: 182 cm
Geraldine: 153 cm
Difference: 29 cm

1. Georgina: 195 cm
   Gordon: 142 cm
   Difference: ☐ cm

2. Guang: 178 cm
   Gabrielle: 133 cm
   Difference: ☐ cm

3. Grace: 168 cm
   George: 149 cm
   Difference: ☐ cm

4. Geeti: 184 cm
   Gus: 157 cm
   Difference: ☐ cm

5. Gogal: 150 cm
   Gloria: 176 cm
   Difference: ☐ cm

6. Guilia: 168 cm
   Gideon: 185 cm
   Difference: ☐ cm

7. Gonzalo: 174 cm
   Gimbaya: 183 cm
   Difference: ☐ cm

8. Giovanna: 203 cm
   Gilbert: 156 cm
   Difference: ☐ cm

Today I scored ☐ out of 8.

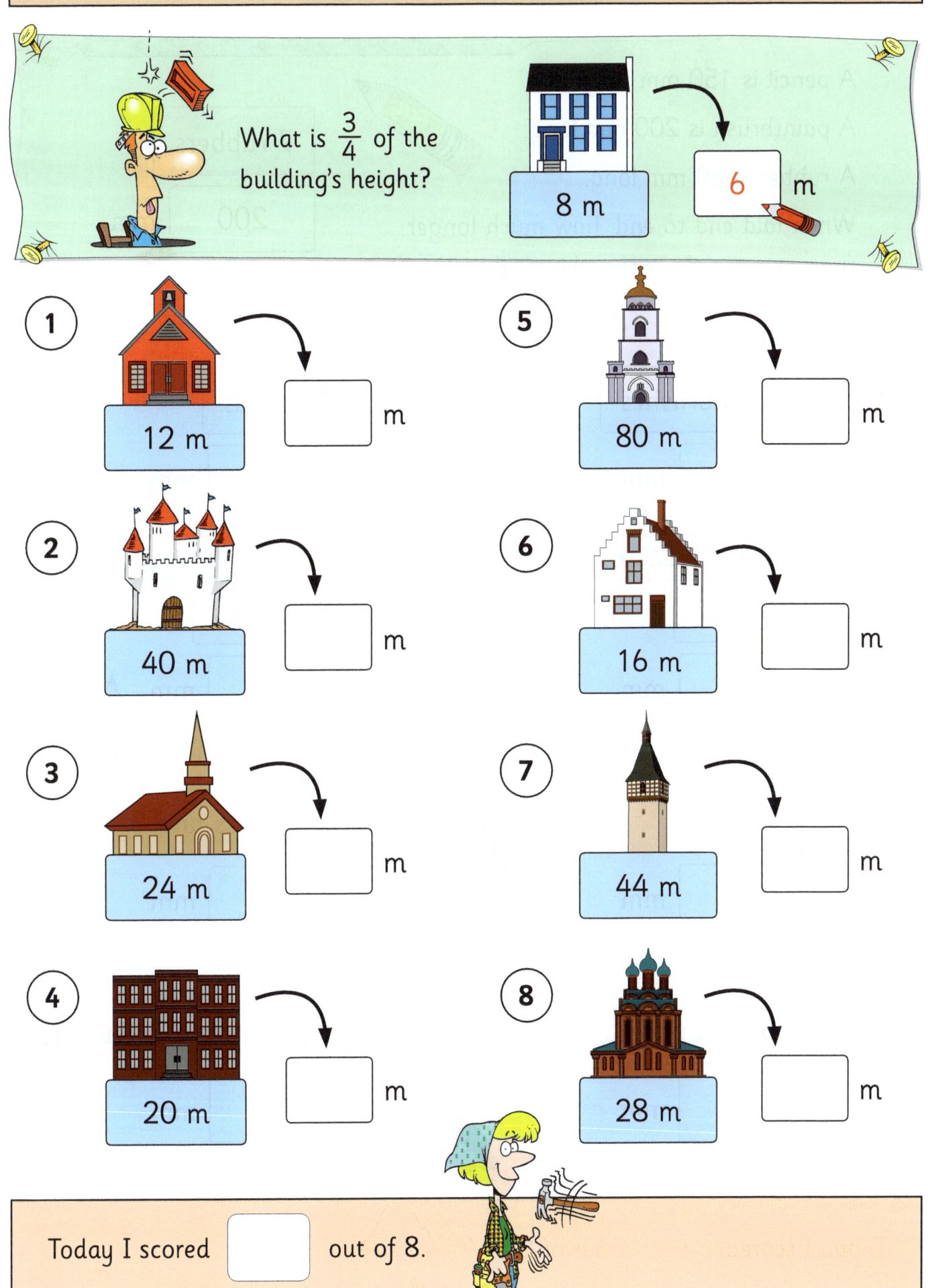

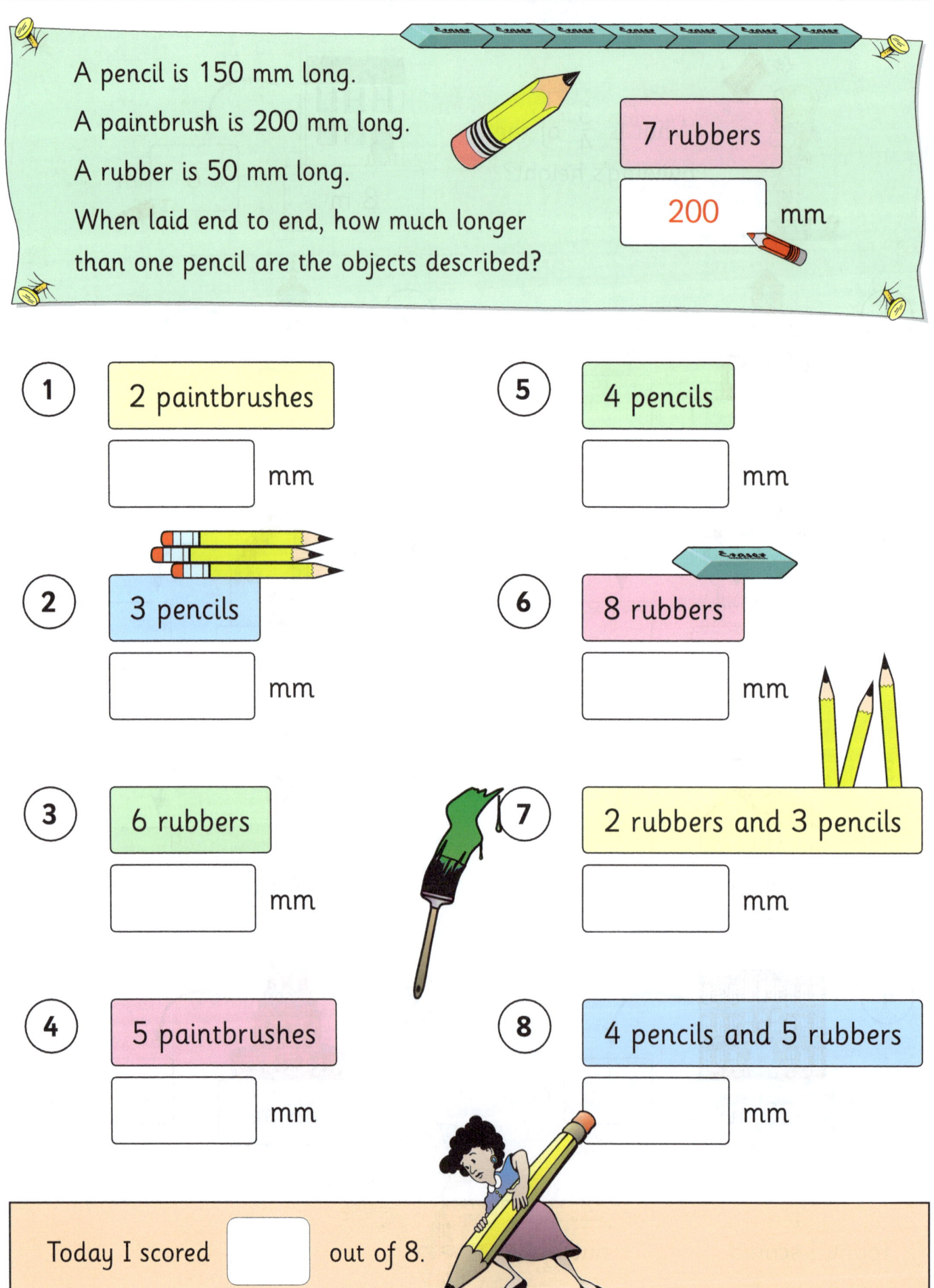

Week 5 — Day 1

Put these numbers in order, starting with the **largest**.

42   89   539   604   134

| 604 | 539 | 134 | 89 | 42 |

1) 91   156   361   705   588

2) 95   659   511   741   362

3) 473   290   79   412   67

4) 332   355   92   279   180

5) 43   667   687   34   768

6) 527   525   225   257   653

Today I scored ☐ out of 6.

Week 5 — Day 2

Use the calculation shown to write the missing number in the box.

724 + 231 = 955

955 − **231** = 724

1) 461 + 509 = 970

970 − 509 = ☐

2) 564 − 197 = 367

367 + ☐ = 564

3) 397 + 338 = 735

☐ − 397 = 338

4) 836 − 283 = 553

836 − ☐ = 283

5) 199 + 656 = 855

☐ + 199 = 855

6) 389 − 213 = 176

213 + ☐ = 389

7) 438 + 524 = 962

962 − ☐ = 438

8) 742 − 591 = 151

☐ + 151 = 742

Today I scored ☐ out of 8.

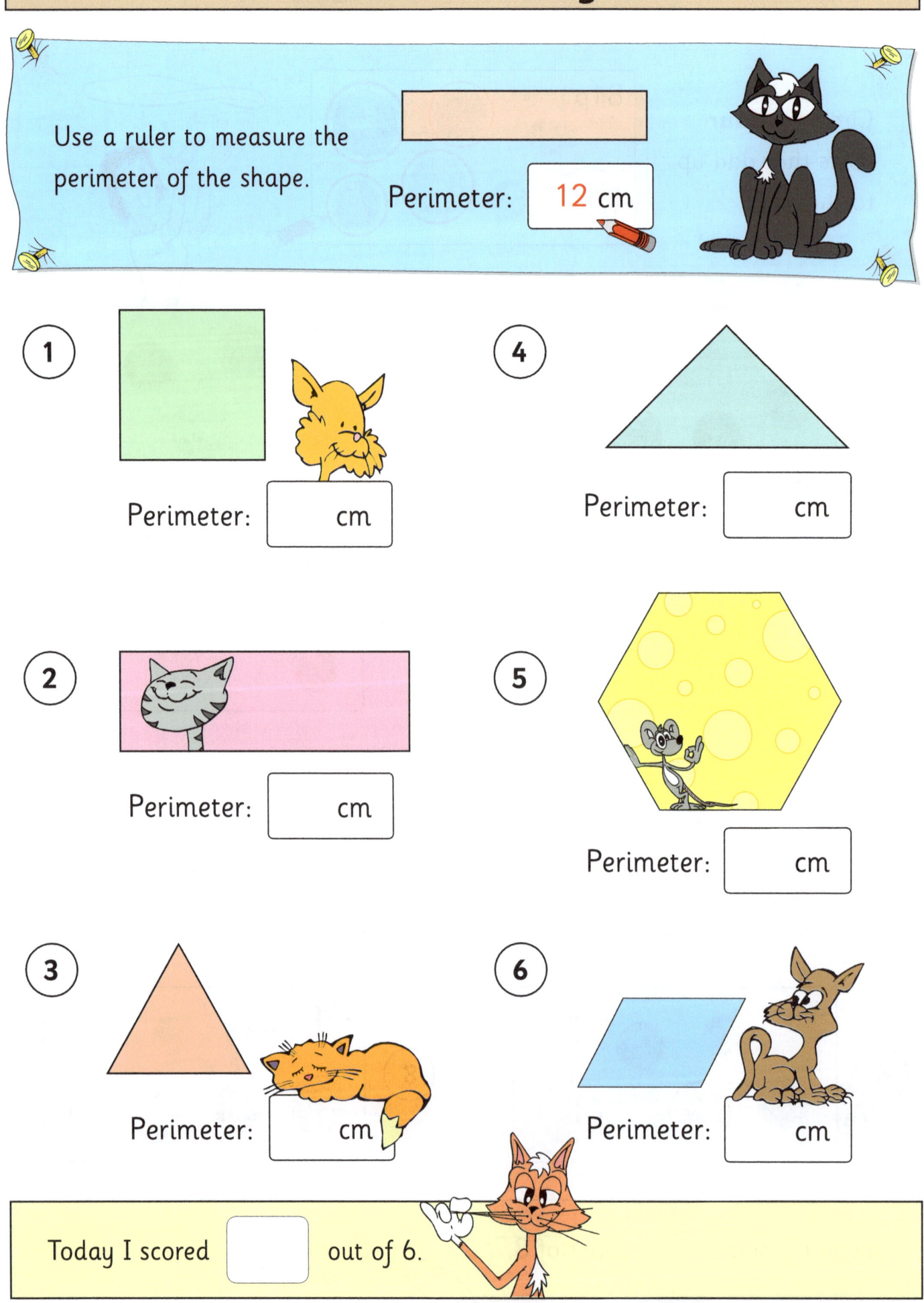

Week 5 — Day 5

Amelia and Sadiq share some money. Use the information to work out how much money Sadiq gets.

They have £43. Amelia gets £3 more than Sadiq.

Sadiq gets £20

1. They have £54. Amelia gets £10 more than Sadiq.

   Sadiq gets £

2. They have £19. Amelia gets £9 more than Sadiq.

   Sadiq gets £

3. They have £28. Amelia gets £4 more than Sadiq.

   Sadiq gets £

4. They have £32. Amelia gets £12 more than Sadiq.

   Sadiq gets £

5. They have £27. Amelia gets £5 more than Sadiq.

   Sadiq gets £

6. They have £45. Amelia gets £9 more than Sadiq.

   Sadiq gets £

7. They have £63. Amelia gets £13 more than Sadiq.

   Sadiq gets £

8. They have £75. Amelia gets £17 more than Sadiq.

   Sadiq gets £

Today I scored ☐ out of 8.

Week 6 — Day 1

Sadie records the number of paint pots she has in a pictogram. Complete the pictogram.

She has 6 red paint pots.

Blue	○○
Green	○
Red	○○○

Key: ○ = 2

1) She has 10 black paint pots.

Red	□□□
Green	□□
Black	

Key: □ = 2

2) She has 10 brown paint pots.

Black	✗✗✗✗
White	✗
Brown	

Key: ✗ = 5

3) She has 30 blue paint pots.

Red	○○○○
Blue	
Pink	○○

Key: ○ = 10

4) She has 12 yellow paint pots.

Yellow	
Orange	△△
Pink	△

Key: △ = 3

5) She has 25 black paint pots.

White	○○○○
Black	
Blue	○○

Key: ○ = 5

6) She has 16 yellow paints pots.

Yellow	
Blue	□□□
Green	□□□

Key: □ = 4

7) She has 15 red paint pots.

Yellow	△
White	△△
Red	

Key: △ = 3

8) She has 20 green paint pots.

Green	
Pink	✗✗✗✗✗✗
White	✗✗✗✗

Key: ✗ = 4

Today I scored ☐ out of 8.

Week 6 — Day 2

What is double the number on the card? 14 → 28

1. 11
2. 23
3. 35
4. 46
5. 29
6. 62
7. 74
8. 55
9. 87
10. 98

Today I scored ☐ out of 10.

Week 6 — Day 3

Circle all the times on the digital clocks that are between 4 o'clock in the afternoon and midnight.

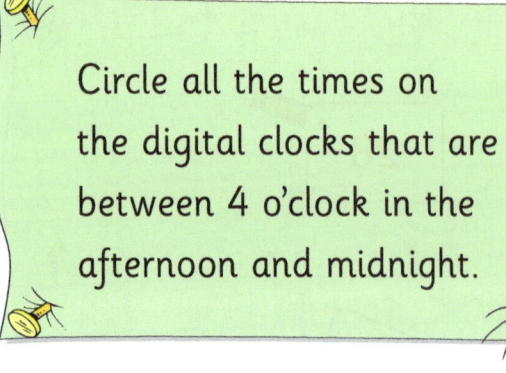

(18:00) 01:00
08:00 (22:00)

1) 02:00 20:00
    13:00 05:00

2) 17:00 10:00
    21:00 14:00

3) 19:20 22:50
    02:10 09:30

4) 16:20 15:40
    19:30 23:10

5) 23:55 10:05
    04:25 20:35

6) 01:31 21:45
    09:31 18:15

7) 22:14 16:37
    04:44 03:09

8) 15:59 00:01
    16:01 23:59

Today I scored ☐ out of 8.

Week 6 — Day 4

Aysha recorded the birds she saw in a pictogram. Complete the sentence.

Herons	◐
Swans	◯
Ducks	◯◯◯
Geese	◯

Key: ◯ = 4 birds

There were [2] more swans than herons.

1

Robins	◯◐
Pigeons	◯◯
Blackbirds	◯◯◯◯
Magpies	◯◯

There were [ ] more magpies than robins.

2

Crows	◯◯◯
Swans	◯◯◯◐
Blackbirds	◯◯◯
Robins	◯

There were [ ] fewer robins than swans.

3

Crows	◯◯◯◯
Swans	◯◯◐
Magpies	◯◯◯◯
Herons	◯◐

There were [ ] more swans than herons.

4

Crows	◯◯◯◐
Magpies	◯◯◐
Ducks	◯◯◯
Herons	◯◐

There were [ ] fewer ducks than crows.

5

Pigeons	◯◯◯◐
Geese	◯◯◯◯◐
Swans	◯◯◐
Ducks	◯◯◯◯◯

There were [ ] more geese than swans.

6

Robins	◯◯◯
Pigeons	◯◯
Ducks	◯◯◯◯◐
Magpies	◯◯◐

There were [ ] fewer pigeons than ducks.

Today I scored [ ] out of 6.

Week 6 — Day 5

Look at the items and their prices.

How much change does Jazz get from £1?

Jazz buys two sweets and one chocolate bar.

Change = 58p

1

Jazz buys one sweet and one chocolate bar.

Change = ___ p

2

Jazz buys one sweet and two chocolate bars.

Change = ___ p

3

Jazz buys five sweets and one chocolate bar.

Change = ___ p

4

Jazz buys one sweet and two chocolate bars.

Change = ___ p

5

Jazz buys one sweet and two chocolate bars.

Change = ___ p

6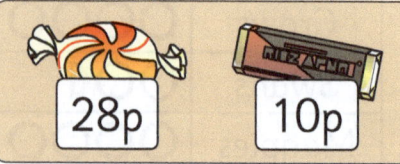

Jazz buys two sweets and one chocolate bar.

Change = ___ p

Today I scored ___ out of 6.

Week 7 — Day 1

Circle all the numbers that match the description in the box.

a hundreds digit higher than 2

| 95 | (376) | 259 | (504) |
| 122 | (443) | (312) | 28 |

1) a hundreds digit lower than 4

| 208 | 321 | 729 | 403 |
| 44 | 527 | 458 | 222 |

4) a hundreds digit higher than 3

| 335 | 533 | 129 | 288 |
| 596 | 254 | 664 | 185 |

2) a hundreds digit higher than 6

| 752 | 528 | 841 | 369 |
| 973 | 419 | 715 | 466 |

5) a hundreds digit higher than 8

| 196 | 781 | 274 | 934 |
| 328 | 945 | 906 | 123 |

3) a hundreds digit lower than 7

| 471 | 745 | 811 | 636 |
| 573 | 333 | 970 | 959 |

6) a hundreds digit lower than 9

| 417 | 988 | 907 | 92 |
| 776 | 994 | 869 | 174 |

Today I scored ☐ out of 6.

Week 7 — Day 2

Circle the **lighter** mass in each pair.

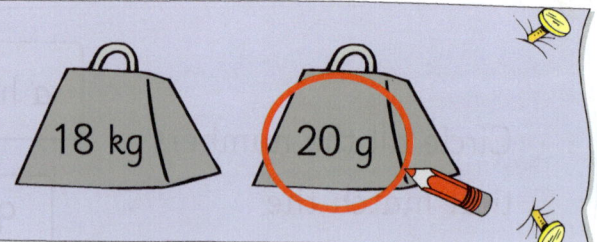

1.
2.
3.
4.
5.
6.

7.
8.
9.
10.
11.
12.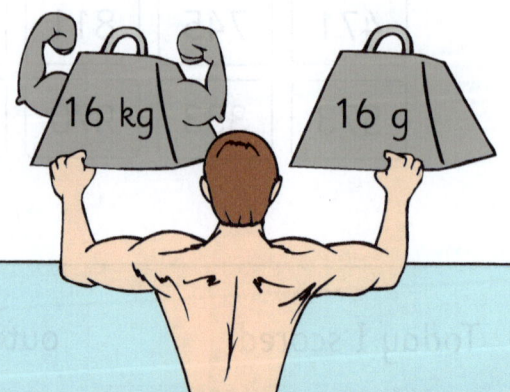

Today I scored ☐ out of 12.

Week 7 — Day 3

How much does the box of fruit or vegetables weigh?

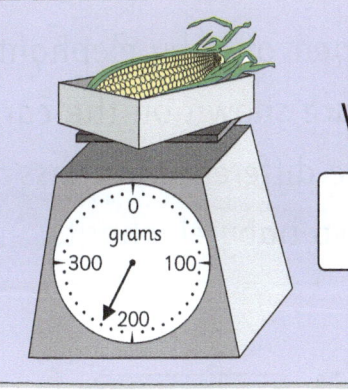

Weight: 230 g

① 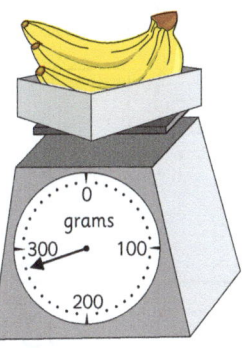 Weight: ____ g

② 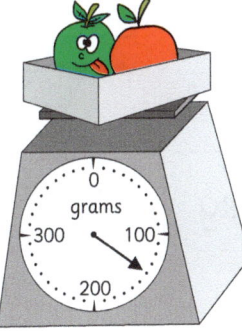 Weight: ____ g

③ 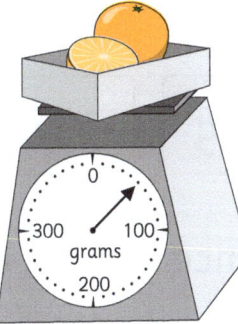 Weight: ____ g

④  Weight: ____ kg

⑤  Weight: ____ kg

⑥ 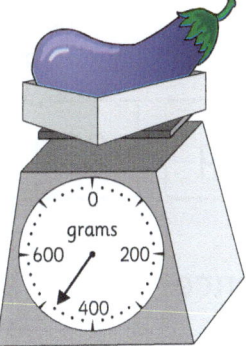 Weight: ____ g

Today I scored ____ out of 6.

Week 7 — Day 4

Will weighs a pair of baby elephants. Their weights are shown on the cards. Write down the difference in mass between the two baby elephants.

160 kg   210 kg

Difference: 50 kg

1) 170 kg   120 kg
Difference: ___ kg

2) 235 kg   210 kg
Difference: ___ kg

3) 195 kg   125 kg
Difference: ___ kg

4) 145 kg   220 kg
Difference: ___ kg

5) 260 kg   118 kg
Difference: ___ kg

6) 136 kg   208 kg
Difference: ___ kg

7) 154 kg   232 kg
Difference: ___ kg

8) 244 kg   187 kg
Difference: ___ kg

Today I scored ___ out of 8.

Week 7 — Day 5

How many people are still at the beach?

46 people are at the beach. Then, 20 people go home. Later, 28 new people arrive and 7 more people go home.

47

1) 45 people are at the beach. Soon, 15 people go home. Later, 31 new people arrive and 5 more people go home.

2) 34 people are at the beach. Soon, 24 people go home. Later, 15 new people arrive and 13 more people go home.

3) 54 people are at the beach. Soon, 12 people go home. Later, 16 new people arrive and 27 more people go home.

4) 76 people are at the beach. Soon, 29 people go home. Later, 23 new people arrive and 15 more people go home.

5) 61 people are at the beach. Soon, 13 people go home. Later, 29 new people arrive and 17 more people go home.

6) 53 people are at the beach. Soon, 26 people go home. Later, 19 new people arrive and 28 more people go home.

Today I scored ☐ out of 6.

Week 8 — Day 1

How many degrees does the temperature need to change by to reach the value in the yellow box?

5 °C   Change = 15 °C

1)  25 °C   Change = ☐ °C

2) 30 °C   Change = ☐ °C

3) 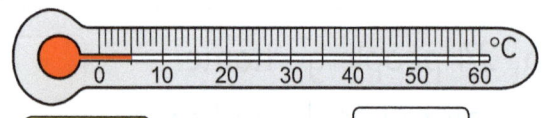 40 °C   Change = ☐ °C

4) 24 °C   Change = ☐ °C

5) 33 °C   Change = ☐ °C

6) 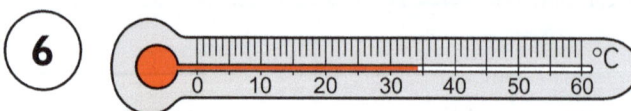 18 °C   Change = ☐ °C

7) 35 °C   Change = ☐ °C

8) 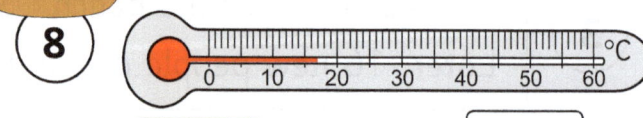 41 °C   Change = ☐ °C

9) 19 °C   Change = ☐ °C

10) 28 °C   Change = ☐ °C

Today I scored ☐ out of 10.

Year 3 Maths — Spring Term

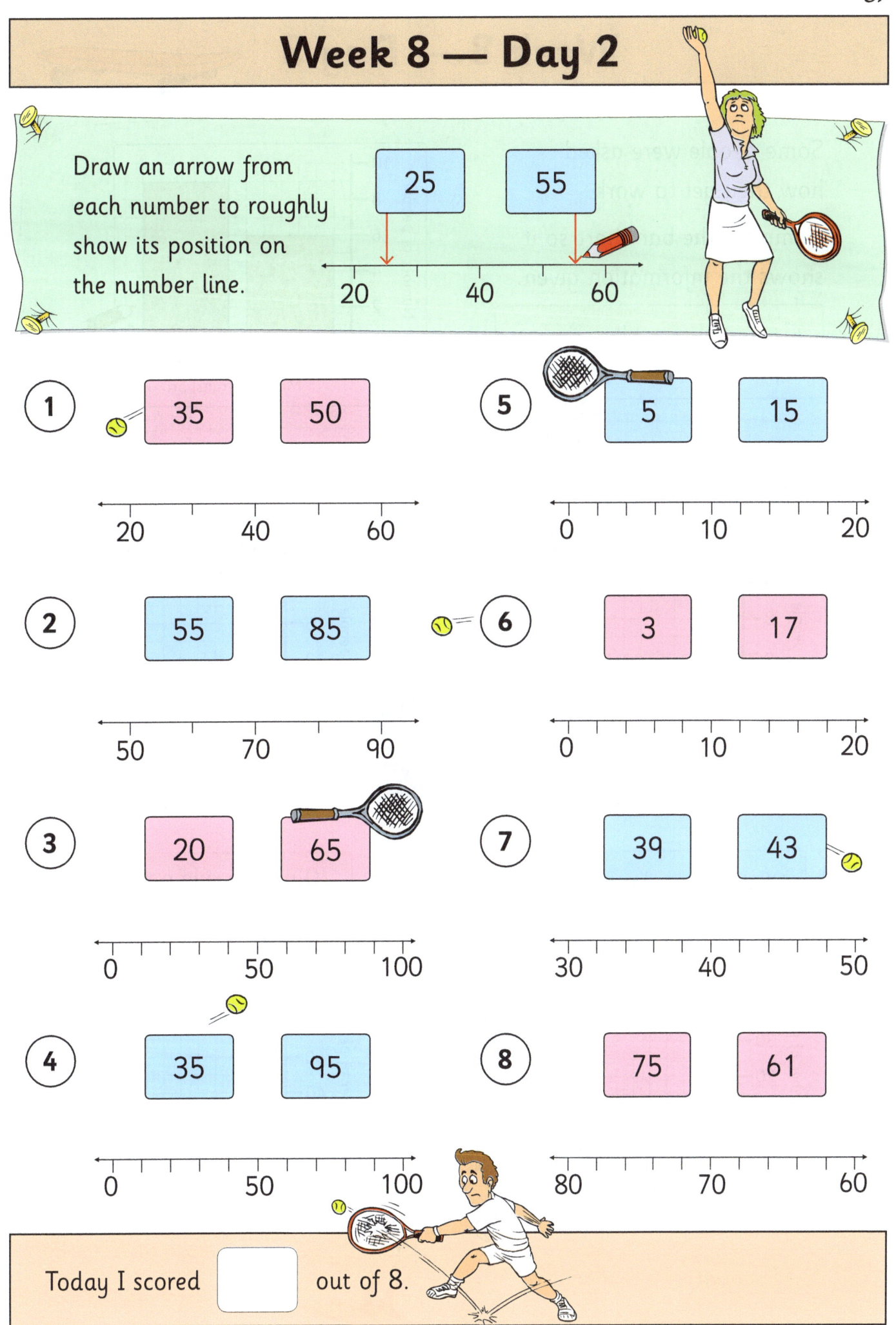

Week 8 — Day 3

Some people were asked how they get to work.

Complete the bar chart so it shows the information given.

6 people use a bike.
9 people use a skateboard.

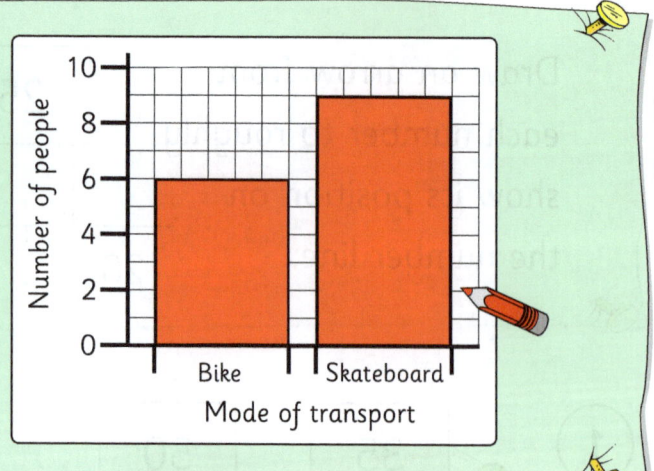

1) 9 people use a car.
3 people use a bus.

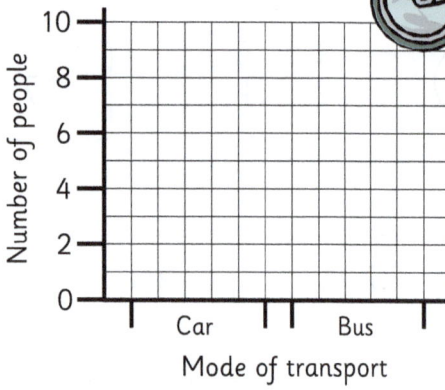

3) 18 people use a boat.
10 people use a plane.
14 people get a train.

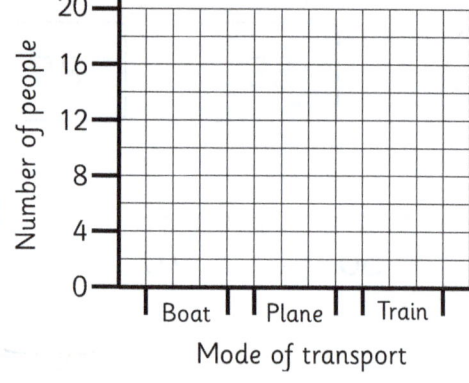

2) 25 people roller blade.
35 people use a scooter.

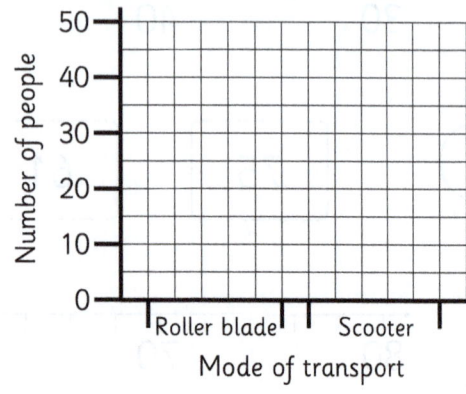

4) 70 people ride a donkey.
50 people ride a horse.
35 people ride a camel.

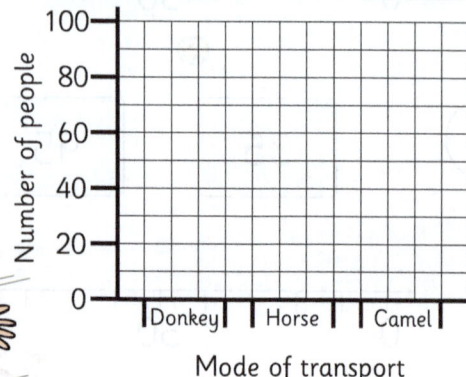

Today I scored ☐ out of 4.

Week 8 — Day 4

How many of the films were **not** action films or comedy films?

A cinema showed 165 films. They showed 40 action films. They showed 50 more comedy films than action films. **35**

1. A cinema showed 220 films. They showed 40 action films. They showed 30 more comedy films than action films.

2. A cinema showed 185 films. They showed 35 action films. They showed 65 more comedy films than action films.

3. A cinema showed 254 films. They showed 30 action films. They showed 65 more comedy films than action films.

4. A cinema showed 180 films. They showed 62 action films. They showed 15 more comedy films than action films.

5. A cinema showed 231 films. They showed 55 action films. They showed 28 more comedy films than action films.

6. A cinema showed 283 films. They showed 46 action films. They showed 37 more comedy films than action films.

Today I scored ☐ out of 6.

Week 8 — Day 5

Use the information in the bar chart to answer the questions.

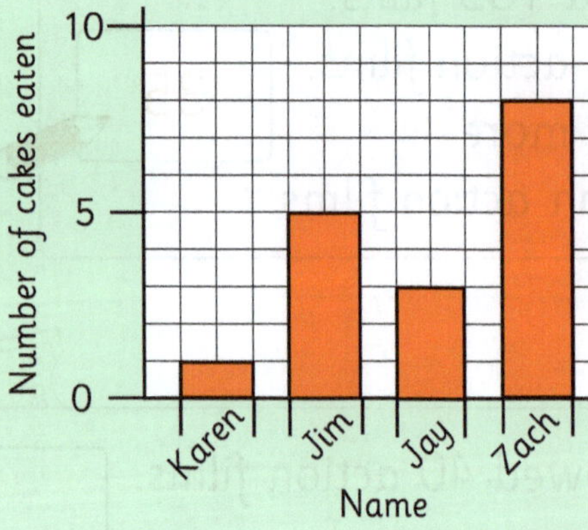

How many **more** cakes did Jim eat than Karen? **4**

How many **fewer** cakes did Jay eat than Zach? **5**

1 How many **more** cakes did Obasi eat than Tom?

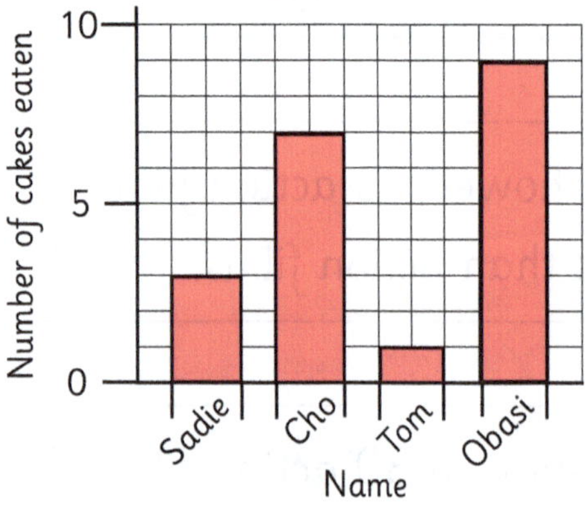

How many **fewer** cakes did Sadie eat than Cho?

2 How many **more** cakes did Rowan eat than Will?

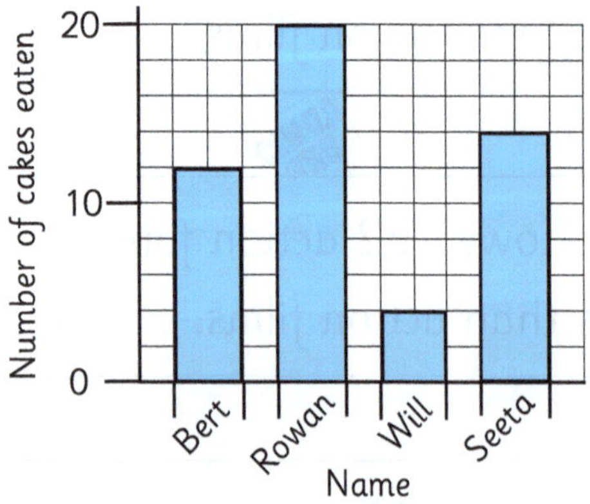

How many **fewer** cakes did Bert eat than Seeta?

3 How many **more** cakes did Sadiq eat than Amy?

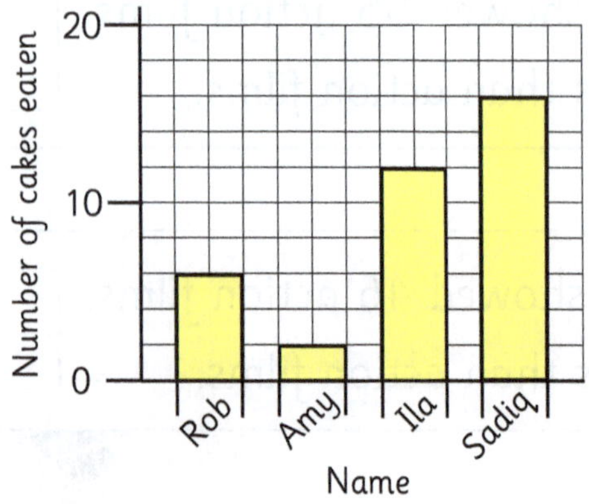

How many **fewer** cakes did Rob eat than Ila?

Today I scored ☐ out of 3.

Week 9 — Day 1

Use your times tables to complete the calculations.

10 x 5 = 50

1) 5 x 3 =

2) 4 x 8 =

3) 14 x 10 =

4) 25 ÷ 5 =

5) 15 x 4 =

6) 21 ÷ 3 =

7) 5 x 11 =

8) 46 ÷ 2 =

9) 3 x 20 =

10) 28 ÷ 4 =

11) 14 x 5 =

12) 36 ÷ 3 =

Today I scored [ ] out of 12.

Week 9 — Day 2

Look at the time each snail took to finish a race.

Cross out the slowest snail. Circle the quickest snail.

 3 minutes and 45 seconds

 4 minutes and 15 seconds

 6 minutes and 15 seconds

1

 5 minutes and 14 seconds

 7 minutes and 1 second

 6 minutes and 25 seconds

 3 minutes and 50 seconds

2

 2 minutes and 59 seconds

 4 minutes and 36 seconds

 5 minutes and 28 seconds

 4 minutes and 48 seconds

3

 5 minutes and 10 seconds

 4 minutes and 55 seconds

 3 minutes and 45 seconds

 3 minutes and 15 seconds

4

 7 minutes and 18 seconds

 8 minutes and 48 seconds

 6 minutes and 2 seconds

 8 minutes and 39 seconds

5

 3 minutes and 20 seconds

 5 minutes and 7 seconds

 3 minutes and 19 seconds

 4 minutes and 11 seconds

Today I scored 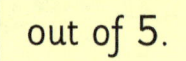 out of 5.

Year 3 Maths — Spring Term

Week 9 — Day 3

A person walks the same distance every month for a number of months. How far did they walk each month?

Rose walked 50 km in 5 months.

10 km each month.

1) Haf walked 60 km in 10 months.
☐ km each month.

2) Mae walked 10 km in 2 months.
☐ km each month.

3) Abe walked 20 km in 5 months.
☐ km each month.

4) Pam walked 18 km in 2 months.
☐ km each month.

5) Rad walked 15 km in 3 months.
☐ km each month.

6) Jen walked 16 km in 4 months.
☐ km each month.

7) Wan walked 27 km in 3 months.
☐ km each month.

8) Ron walked 32 km in 4 months.
☐ km each month.

9) Al walked 44 km in 11 months.
☐ km each month.

10) Obe walked 36 km in 3 months.
☐ km each month.

Today I scored ☐ out of 10.

Week 9 — Day 4

Write down the calculation you would need to do to answer the question.

Jason has 24 apples. He gives half of them away. How many apples does he give away?

24 ÷ 2

1) 8 orange trees each grow 10 oranges. How many oranges are there in total?

2) There are 4 pies. Each pie is cut into 8 pieces. How many pieces of pie are there in total?

3) Valeria makes 2 socks every hour. How many hours would it take her to make 80 socks?

4) There are 5 judo classes. There are 12 people per class. How many people are there in total?

5) A grocer shares 60 carrots equally between 3 bags. How many carrots go in each bag?

6) A baker bakes 50 loaves of bread a day. How many loaves does she bake in 2 days?

7) A postman travels 80 miles every day. How far will he have travelled after 5 days?

8) A 54 cm piece of ribbon is cut into 6 equal pieces. How long is each piece of ribbon?

Today I scored ☐ out of 8.

Week 9 — Day 5

Lola and George want to buy the same number of biscuits. Write the answer in the box.

Lola buys 4 packs of 5 biscuits. How many packs of 10 biscuits should George buy? **2**

1. Lola buys 3 packs of 8 biscuits. How many packs of 6 biscuits should George buy?

2. Lola buys 10 packs of 3 biscuits. How many packs of 5 biscuits should George buy?

3. Lola buys 4 packs of 12 biscuits. How many packs of 8 biscuits should George buy?

4. Lola buys 5 packs of 8 biscuits. How many packs of 10 biscuits should George buy?

5. Lola buys 15 packs of 4 biscuits. How many packs of 6 biscuits should George buy?

6. Lola buys 11 packs of 8 biscuits. How many packs of 4 biscuits should George buy?

7. Lola buys 8 packs of 20 biscuits. How many packs of 16 biscuits should George buy?

Today I scored ☐ out of 7.

Week 10 — Day 1

Fill in the missing numbers, counting in steps of eight.　　0　8　16　24　32

1)　24　32　☐　☐　☐

2)　40　48　☐　☐　☐

3)　56　☐　72　☐　☐

4)　☐　24　☐　☐　48

5)　80　72　☐　☐　☐

6)　☐　☐　☐　40　48

7)　32　☐　16　☐　☐

8)　56　☐　☐　☐　24

9)　80　88　☐　☐　☐

10)　96　☐　☐　☐　64

Today I scored ☐ out of 10.

Week 10 — Day 2

Put these numbers in order, starting with the **smallest**.

427, 100, 720, 248, 575

100, 248, 427, 575, 720

1) 103, 730, 595, 373, 970

103, 373, 595, 730, 970

2) 800, 571, 678, 233, 760

233, 571, 678, 760, 800

3) 357, 106, 945, 167, 495

106, 167, 357, 495, 945

4) 453, 242, 728, 765, 278

242, 278, 453, 728, 765

5) 835, 687, 568, 508, 386

386, 508, 568, 687, 835

6) 759, 798, 547, 574, 745

547, 574, 745, 759, 798

Today I scored ☐ out of 6.

Week 10 — Day 4

This is a bakery's menu:

bread roll	50p
cupcake	75p
doughnut	£1.00
sandwich	£1.50

Ranjit has £2.
He buys one cupcake.

His change = £1.25

Calculate the shopper's change.

1 Tess has £2.
She buys one sandwich.

Her change = £ ⬚

2 Milo has £5.
He buys one bread roll and one sandwich.

His change = £ ⬚

3 Roberta has £2.
She buys one cupcake and one doughnut

Her change = £ ⬚

4 Diego has £5.
He buys two sandwiches.

His change = £ ⬚

5 Grant has £10.
He buys two doughnuts and one bread roll.

His change = £ ⬚

6 Mia has £10.
She buys two cupcakes and two sandwiches.

Her change = £ ⬚

Today I scored ⬚ out of 6.

Week 10 — Day 5

A herd of camels is in the desert. Some camels go to the sand dunes. Some camels stay where they are. The remaining camels go to an oasis. How many camels are in the oasis?

There are 50 camels in the herd. 22 go to the sand dunes and 18 stay where they are. → 10

1. There are 78 camels in the herd. 38 go to the sand dunes and 10 stay where they are.

2. There are 43 camels in the herd. 21 go to the sand dunes and 12 stay where they are.

3. There are 65 camels in the herd. 14 go to the sand dunes and 30 stay where they are.

4. There are 87 camels in the herd. 55 go to the sand dunes and 24 stay where they are.

5. There are 99 camels in the herd. 46 go to the sand dunes and 35 stay where they are.

6. There are 91 camels in the herd. 27 go to the sand dunes and 38 stay where they are.

Today I scored ☐ out of 6.

Week 11 — Day 1

The table shows how many times 3 people went swimming in 3 months.

Circle the name of the person who went swimming the **most** times overall. Write how many **more** times Kala went swimming than Baz in **June**.

Name	May	June	July
Baz	4	3	5
Kala	5	6	2
(Anisa)	2	9	6

 3

1.

Name	May	June	July
Baz	3	4	7
Kala	5	6	2
Anisa	7	7	1

5.

Name	May	June	July
Baz	17	16	9
Kala	11	24	5
Anisa	6	7	12

2.

Name	May	June	July
Baz	2	6	2
Kala	3	9	4
Anisa	3	1	5

6.

Name	May	June	July
Baz	11	8	12
Kala	20	15	12
Anisa	9	3	14

3.

Name	May	June	July
Baz	7	5	8
Kala	3	9	5
Anisa	11	3	4

7.

Name	May	June	July
Baz	12	21	18
Kala	16	27	7
Anisa	4	9	4

4.

Name	May	June	July
Baz	3	12	6
Kala	9	17	2
Anisa	10	11	12

8.

Name	May	June	July
Baz	23	19	9
Kala	11	28	14
Anisa	17	13	5

Today I scored [ ] out of 8.

Week 11 — Day 2

Complete the fraction to show how much of the shape has been shaded.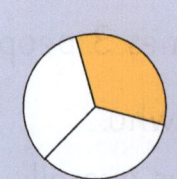

1. 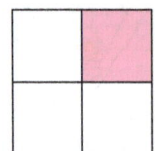 $\dfrac{1}{}$

2. 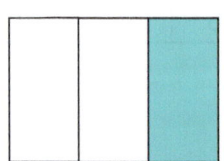 $\dfrac{1}{}$

3.  $\dfrac{1}{}$

4.  $\dfrac{1}{}$

5. 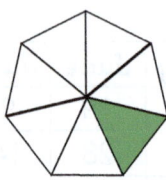 $\dfrac{1}{}$

6. 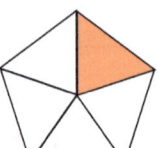 $\dfrac{1}{}$

7.  $\dfrac{1}{}$

8. 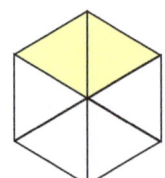 $\dfrac{1}{}$

9. 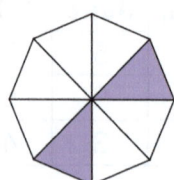 $\dfrac{1}{}$

10. 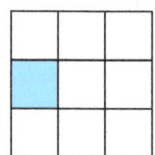 $\dfrac{1}{}$

Today I scored ☐ out of 10.

Week 11 — Day 3

Complete the sentence using =, < or >.   Four hundred [>] 300

1) 500 [ ] Six hundred

2) Two hundred and twenty [ ] 150

3) Four hundred and seventy [ ] 470

4) 330 [ ] Three hundred and ten

5) 561 [ ] Five hundred and sixty one

6) Seven hundred and forty five [ ] 598

7) Nine hundred and twenty three [ ] 875

8) 657 [ ] Six hundred and fifty seven

9) 782 [ ] Seven hundred and ninety

10) 877 [ ] Eight hundred and seventy seven

11) Six hundred and four [ ] 614

12) 968 [ ] Nine hundred and eighty six

Today I scored [ ] out of 12.

Week 11 — Day 4

Complete the sentence by writing the correct fraction.   3 is $\frac{1}{2}$ of 6

1) 4 is ⬚ of 12

2) 5 is ⬚ of 20

3) 6 is ⬚ of 18

4) 11 is ⬚ of 22

5) 8 is ⬚ of 32

6) 7 is ⬚ of 35

7) 5 is ⬚ of 40

8) 5 is ⬚ of 30

9) 10 is ⬚ of 100

10) 3 is ⬚ of 27

11) 8 is ⬚ of 64

12) 9 is ⬚ of 45

Today I scored ⬚ out of 12.

Week 11 — Day 5

Write down how many scarves Nora knits.

$\frac{1}{4}$ of a bag of wool makes one scarf.
Nora uses the number of bags shown.

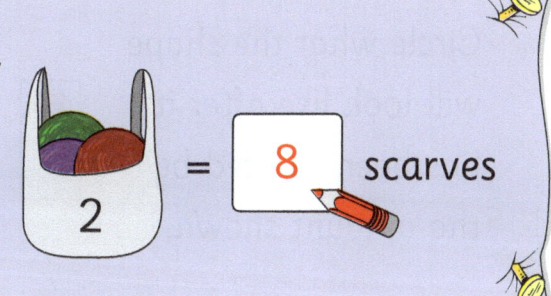 = 8 scarves

1) $\frac{1}{4}$ of a bag of wool makes one scarf.
Nora uses the number of bags shown.

 = ☐ scarves

2) $\frac{1}{5}$ of a bag of wool makes one scarf.
Nora uses the number of bags shown.

 = ☐ scarves

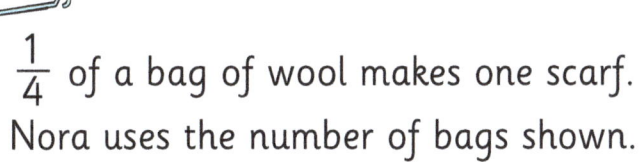 3) $\frac{1}{3}$ of a bag of wool makes one scarf.
Nora uses the number of bags shown.

 = ☐ scarves

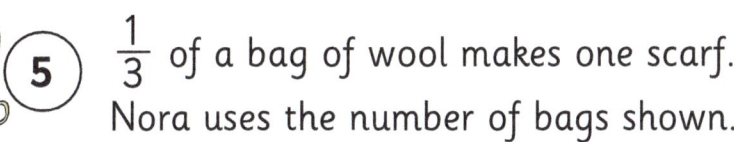 4) $\frac{1}{4}$ of a bag of wool makes one scarf.
Nora uses the number of bags shown.

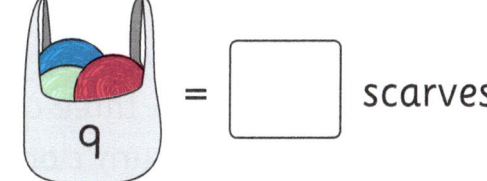 = ☐ scarves

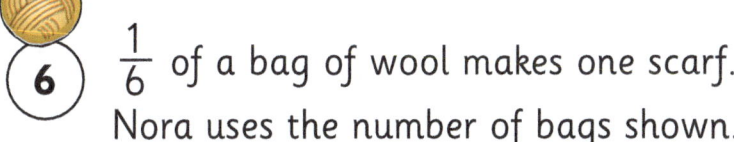 5) $\frac{1}{3}$ of a bag of wool makes one scarf.
Nora uses the number of bags shown.

 = ☐ scarves

6) $\frac{1}{6}$ of a bag of wool makes one scarf.
Nora uses the number of bags shown.

= ☐ scarves

Today I scored ☐ out of 6.

Week 12 — Day 1

Circle what the shape will look like after it has been rotated by the amount shown.

A half turn clockwise

1. A half turn anti-clockwise

2. A half turn clockwise

3. A quarter turn clockwise

4. A quarter turn anti-clockwise

5. A three quarter turn anti-clockwise

6. A three quarter turn clockwise

7. A three quarter turn anti-clockwise

Today I scored ☐ out of 7.

Year 3 Maths — Spring Term

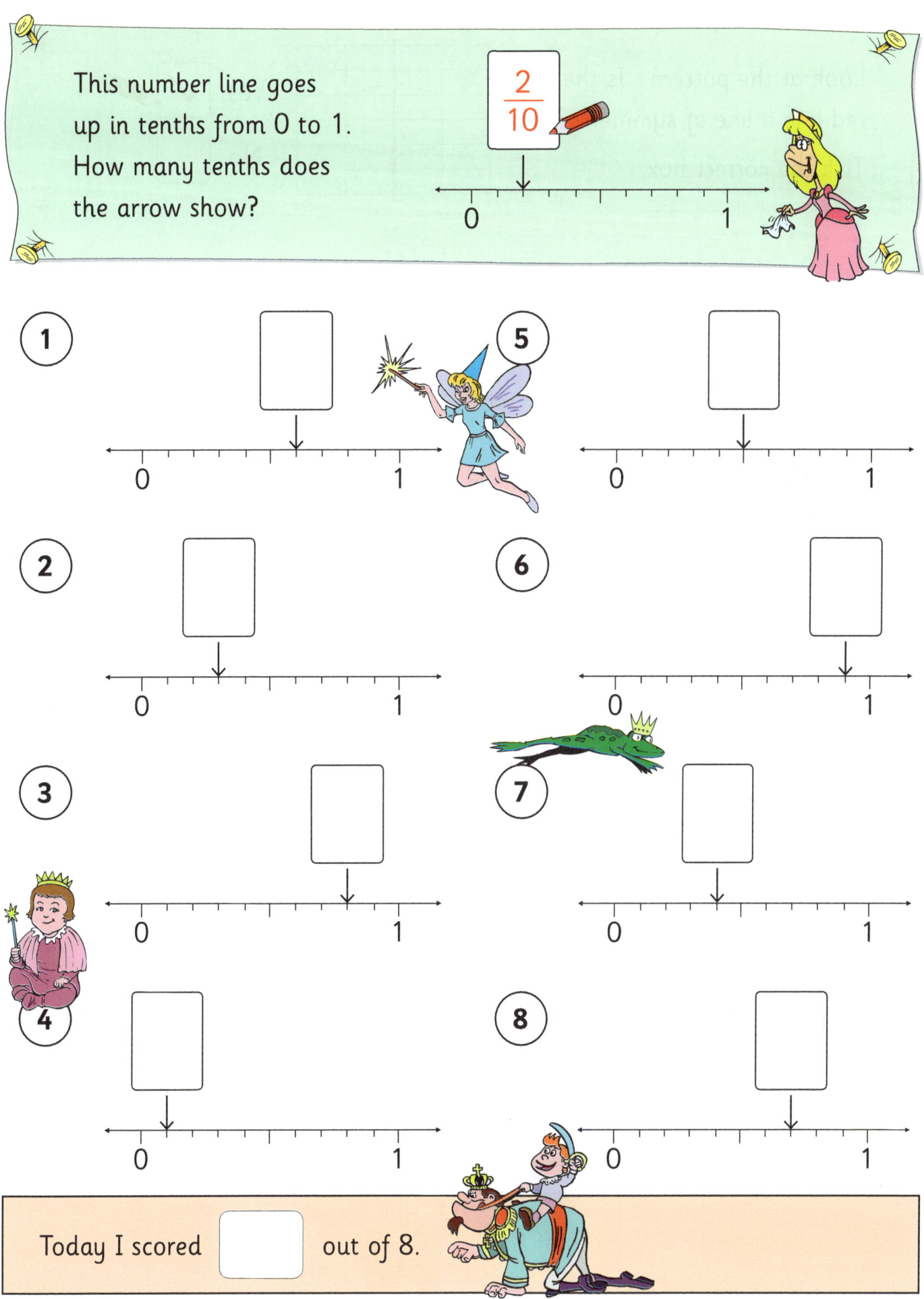

Week 12 — Day 3

Look at the pattern. Is the red line a line of symmetry? Tick the correct box.

Yes ✓
No

1. Yes ☐ No ☐

2. Yes ☐ No ☐

3. Yes ☐ No ☐

4. Yes ☐ No ☐

5. Yes ☐ No ☐

6. Yes ☐ No ☐

7. Yes ☐ No ☐

8. Yes ☐ No ☐

Today I scored ☐ out of 8.

Year 3 Maths — Spring Term

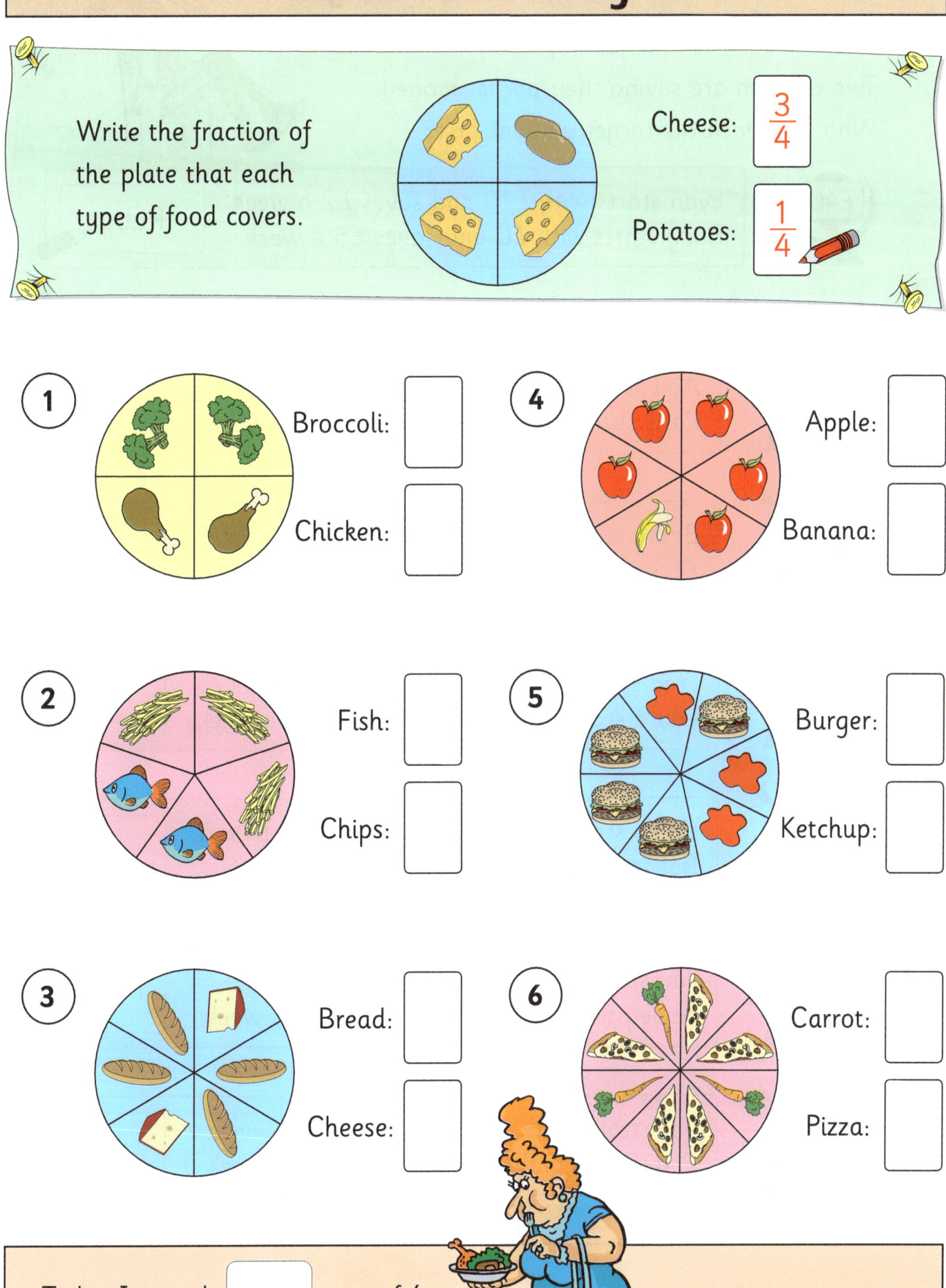

Week 12 — Day 5

Two children are saving their pocket money.
Who will reach the target amount first?

Evan starts with £10 and saves £2 a week.
Ruby starts with £0 and saves £5 a week.

Ruby

1.  Abu starts with £0 and saves £4 a week.
Paris starts with £18 and saves £2 a week.

2.  Becky starts with £10 and saves £5 a week.
Zack starts with £0 and saves £8 a week.

3.  Fred starts with £3 and saves £8 a week.
Laura starts with £14 and saves £3 a week.

4.  Caleb starts with £10 and saves £5 a week.
Bai starts with £5 and saves £10 a week.

5.  Jay starts with £4 and saves £8 a week.
Abbey starts with £8 and saves £5 a week.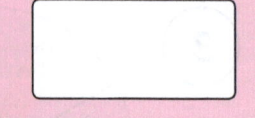

6.  Tom starts with £12 and saves £8 a week.
Page starts with £25 and saves £4 a week.

Today I scored ☐ out of 6.

Year 3 Maths — Spring Term © CGP — Not to be photocopied

Answers

Week 1 — Day 1
1. 12
2. 10
3. 6
4. 9
5. 11
6. 5
7. 7
8. 2
9. 3
10. 4
11. 3
12. 4

Week 1 — Day 2
1. Hammers = ||||, 4
   Nails = ||||\|, 6
2. Hammers = |||, 3
   Nails = ||||\||, 7
3. Hammers = ||||\, 5
   Nails = ||||\||, 7
4. Hammers = ||||\|, 6
   Nails = ||||\||||, 9
5. Hammers = ||||\, 5
   Nails = ||||\ ||||\|, 11

Week 1 — Day 3
1. four hundred and sixty seven
2. three hundred and forty six
3. eight hundred and eighteen
4. six hundred and twenty one
5. nine hundred and eighty five
6. seven hundred and ninety nine
7. two hundred and thirty
8. five hundred and four

Week 1 — Day 4
1. 399
2. 898
3. 999
4. 370
5. 403
6. 812
7. 823
8. 432
9. 302
10. 516

Week 1 — Day 5
1. 19
2. 31
3. 35
4. 33
5. 77
6. 53
7. 29
8. 49

Week 2 — Day 1
1. II
2. IV
3. X
4. VII
5. V
6. XII
7. VI
8. VIII
9. XI
10. IX

Week 2 — Day 2
1. 8 < 12
2. 15 < 51
3. 44 > 36
4. 87 < 92
5. 130 > 103
6. 148 > 139
7. 178 < 187
8. 201 < 211
9. 265 > 255
10. 273 > 237
11. 301 < 381
12. 387 > 378

Week 2 — Day 3
1. 400, 700
2. 0, 100
3. 800, 1000
4. 400, 100
5. 1100, 700
6. 500, 0

Week 2 — Day 4
1. 41
2. 112
3. 31
4. 15
5. 218
6. 56
7. 204
8. 19
9. 227
10. 193

Week 2 — Day 5
1. 12
2. 6
3. 9
4. 5
5. 9
6. 9

Week 3 — Day 1
1. 225, 240
2. 435, 444
3. 361, 369
4. 763, 776
5. 517, 531
6. 854, 862
7. 687, 699
8. 898, 911

Week 3 — Day 2
1. 153
2. 349
3. 506
4. 478
5. 643
6. 816
7. 753
8. 820
9. 96
10. 903

Week 3 — Day 3
1. 25
2. 14
3. 24
4. 9
5. 150
6. 29
7. 19
8. 17
9. 55
10. 77

Week 3 — Day 4
1. square-based pyramid
2. cube
3. sphere
4. cone
5. triangle-based pyramid
6. cuboid
7. triangular prism

Week 3 — Day 5
1. 53 + 41 = 94, 41 + 53 = 94,
   51 + 43 = 94 **or** 43 + 51 = 94
2. 61 + 21 = 82 **or** 21 + 61 = 82
3. 82 + 41 = 123, 41 + 82 = 123,
   81 + 42 = 123 **or** 42 + 81 = 123
4. 75 + 62 = 137, 62 + 75 = 137,
   72 + 65 = 137 **or** 65 + 72 = 137
5. 93 + 82 = 175, 82 + 93 = 175,
   92 + 83 = 175 **or** 83 + 92 = 175
6. 75 + 53 = 128, 53 + 75 = 128,
   73 + 55 = 128 **or** 55 + 73 = 128
7. 95 + 71 = 166, 71 + 95 = 166,
   91 + 75 = 166 **or** 75 + 91 = 166
8. 97 + 85 = 182, 85 + 97 = 182,
   95 + 87 = 182 **or** 87 + 95 = 182

Week 4 — Day 1
1. 4 cm
2. 5 cm
3. 2 cm
4. 7 cm
5. 4 cm
6. 3 cm
7. 5 cm
8. 6 cm

Week 4 — Day 2
1. 24 cm
2. 62 m
3. 18 mm
4. 53 cm
5. 72 cm
6. 19 m
7. 98 mm
8. 28 m
9. 42 cm
10. 103 m
11. 99 mm
12. 2 m

Week 4 — Day 3
1. 53 cm
2. 45 cm
3. 19 cm
4. 27 cm
5. 26 cm
6. 17 cm
7. 9 cm
8. 47 cm

Week 4 — Day 4
1. 9 m   5. 60 m
2. 30 m 6. 12 m
3. 18 m 7. 33 m
4. 15 m 8. 21 m

Week 4 — Day 5
1. 250 mm   5. 450 mm
2. 300 mm   6. 250 mm
3. 150 mm   7. 400 mm
4. 850 mm   8. 700 mm

Week 5 — Day 1
1. 705, 588, 361, 156, 91
2. 741, 659, 511, 362, 95
3. 473, 412, 290, 79, 67
4. 355, 332, 279, 180, 92
5. 768, 687, 667, 43, 34
6. 653, 527, 525, 257, 225

Week 5 — Day 2
1. 461   5. 656
2. 197   6. 176
3. 735   7. 524
4. 553   8. 591

Week 5 — Day 3
1.
2.
3.
4.
5.
6.
7.
8.

Week 5 — Day 4
1. 12 cm   4. 12 cm
2. 16 cm   5. 15 cm
3. 9 cm   6. 9 cm

Week 5 — Day 5
1. £22   5. £11
2. £5   6. £18
3. £12   7. £25
4. £10   8. £29

Week 6 — Day 1

1.
Red	☐☐☐
Green	☐☐☐
Black	☐☐☐☐☐

2.
Black	✗✗✗✗
White	✗
Brown	✗✗

3.
Red	○○○○
Blue	○○○
Pink	○○

4.
Yellow	△△△△
Orange	△△
Pink	△

5.
White	○○○○
Black	○○○○○
Blue	○○

6.
Yellow	☐☐☐☐
Blue	☐☐☐
Green	☐☐☐

7.
Yellow	△
White	△△
Red	△△△△△

8.
Green	✗✗✗✗✗
Pink	✗✗✗✗✗✗
White	✗✗✗✗

Week 6 — Day 2
1. 22   6. 124
2. 46   7. 148
3. 70   8. 110
4. 92   9. 174
5. 58   10. 196

Week 6 — Day 3
1. 20:00
2. 17:00 and 21:00
3. 19:20 and 22:50
4. 16:20, 19:30 and 23:10
5. 23:55 and 20:35
6. 21:45 and 18:15
7. 22:14 and 16:37
8. 16:01 and 23:59

Week 6 — Day 4
1. 2   4. 2
2. 10 5. 8
3. 4   6. 10

Week 6 — Day 5
1. 76p   4. 44p
2. 16p   5. 6p
3. 73p   6. 34p

Week 7 — Day 1
1. 208, 321, 44, 222
2. 752, 841, 973, 715
3. 471, 636, 573, 333
4. 533, 596, 664
5. 934, 945, 906
6. 417, 92, 776, 869, 174

Week 7 — Day 2
1. 20 kg   7. 10 g
2. 13 kg   8. 42 g
3. 11 g   9. 37 g
4. 56 kg   10. 56 g
5. 101 g   11. 50 kg
6. 34 g   12. 16 g

Week 7 — Day 3
1. 280 g   4. 1 kg
2. 140 g   5. 5 kg
3. 50 g   6. 480 g

Week 7 — Day 4
1. 50 kg   5. 142 kg
2. 25 kg   6. 72 kg
3. 70 kg   7. 78 kg
4. 75 kg   8. 57 kg

Answers

Week 7 — Day 5
1. 56
2. 12
3. 31
4. 55
5. 60
6. 18

Week 8 — Day 1
1. 10 °C
2. 25 °C
3. 17 °C
4. 20 °C
5. 25 °C
6. 16 °C
7. 17 °C
8. 24 °C
9. 13 °C
10. 28 °C

Week 8 — Day 2

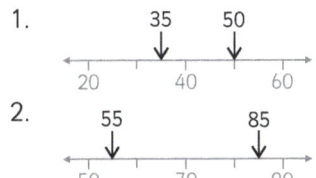

Week 8 — Day 3

1.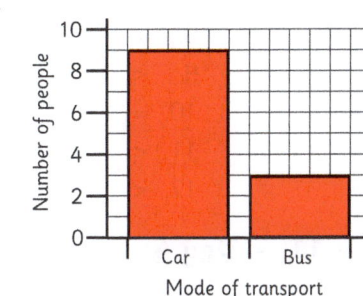

2.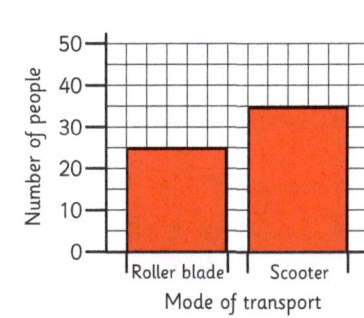

3.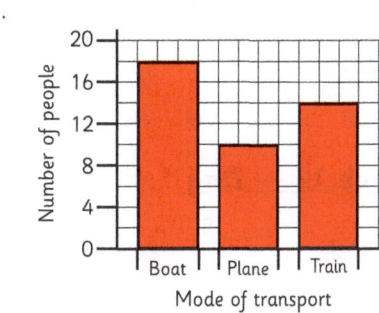

4.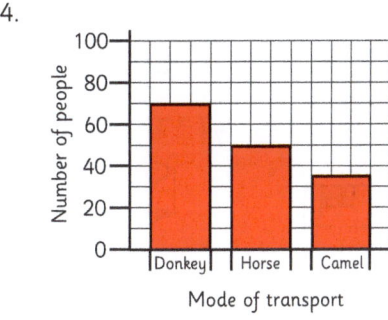

Week 8 — Day 4
1. 110
2. 50
3. 129
4. 41
5. 93
6. 154

Week 8 — Day 5
1. Obasi ate **8** more cakes than Tom.
   Sadie ate **4** fewer cakes than Cho.
2. Rowan ate **16** more cakes than Will.
   Bert ate **2** fewer cakes than Seeta.
3. Sadiq ate **14** more cakes than Amy.
   Rob ate **6** fewer cakes than Ila.

Week 9 — Day 1
1. 15
2. 32
3. 140
4. 5
5. 60
6. 7
7. 55
8. 23
9. 60
10. 7
11. 70
12. 12

Week 9 — Day 2
1. Slowest: 7 minutes and 1 second
   Quickest: 3 minutes and 50 seconds
2. Slowest: 5 minutes and 28 seconds
   Quickest: 2 minutes and 59 seconds
3. Slowest: 5 minutes and 10 seconds
   Quickest: 3 minutes and 15 seconds
4. Slowest: 8 minutes and 48 seconds
   Quickest: 6 minutes and 2 seconds
5. Slowest: 5 minutes and 7 seconds
   Quickest: 3 minutes and 19 seconds

Week 9 — Day 3
1. 6 km
2. 5 km
3. 4 km
4. 9 km
5. 5 km
6. 4 km
7. 9 km
8. 8 km
9. 4 km
10. 12 km

Week 9 — Day 4
1. 8 × 10 or 10 × 8
2. 4 × 8 or 8 × 4
3. 80 ÷ 2
4. 5 × 12 or 12 × 5
5. 60 ÷ 3
6. 50 × 2 or 2 × 50
7. 80 × 5 or 5 × 80
8. 54 ÷ 6

Week 9 — Day 5
1. 4
2. 6
3. 6
4. 4
5. 10
6. 22
7. 10

64

Week 10 — Day 1
1. 24, 32, **40**, **48**, **56**
2. 40, 48, **56**, **64**, **72**
3. 56, **64**, 72, **80**, **88**
4. **16**, 24, **32**, **40**, 48
5. 80, 72, **64**, **56**, **48**
6. **16**, **24**, **32**, 40, 48
7. 32, **24**, 16, **8**, **0**
8. 56, **48**, **40**, **32**, 24
9. 80, 88, **96**, **104**, **112**
10. 96, **88**, **80**, **72**, 64

Week 10 — Day 2
1. 103, 373, 595, 730, 970
2. 233, 571, 678, 760, 800
3. 106, 167, 357, 495, 945
4. 242, 278, 453, 728, 765
5. 386, 508, 568, 687, 835
6. 547, 574, 745, 759, 798

Week 10 — Day 3
1. 40
2. 24
3. 32
4. 80
5. 48
6. 64
7. 56
8. 88
9. 72
10. 96

Week 10 — Day 4
1. £0.50
2. £3.00
3. £0.25
4. £2.00
5. £7.50
6. £5.50

Week 10 — Day 5
1. 30
2. 10
3. 21
4. 8
5. 18
6. 26

Week 11 — Day 1
1. Anisa, 2
2. Kala, 3
3. Baz, 4
4. Anisa, 5
5. Baz, 8
6. Kala, 7
7. Baz, 6
8. Kala, 9

Week 11 — Day 2
1. $\frac{1}{4}$
2. $\frac{1}{3}$
3. $\frac{1}{5}$
4. $\frac{1}{8}$
5. $\frac{1}{7}$
6. $\frac{1}{5}$
7. $\frac{1}{9}$
8. $\frac{1}{3}$
9. $\frac{1}{4}$
10. $\frac{1}{3}$

Week 11 — Day 3
1. <
2. >
3. =
4. >
5. =
6. >
7. >
8. =
9. <
10. =
11. <
12. <

Week 11 — Day 4
1. $\frac{1}{3}$
2. $\frac{1}{4}$
3. $\frac{1}{3}$
4. $\frac{1}{2}$
5. $\frac{1}{4}$
6. $\frac{1}{5}$
7. $\frac{1}{8}$
8. $\frac{1}{6}$
9. $\frac{1}{10}$
10. $\frac{1}{9}$
11. $\frac{1}{8}$
12. $\frac{1}{5}$

Week 11 — Day 5
1. 12
2. 20
3. 21
4. 24
5. 27
6. 48

Week 12 — Day 1
1.
2.
3.
4.
5.
6.
7.

Week 12 — Day 2
1. $\frac{6}{10}$
2. $\frac{3}{10}$
3. $\frac{8}{10}$
4. $\frac{1}{10}$
5. $\frac{5}{10}$
6. $\frac{9}{10}$
7. $\frac{4}{10}$
8. $\frac{7}{10}$

Week 12 — Day 3
1. No
2. Yes
3. No
4. No
5. Yes
6. No
7. Yes
8. No

Week 12 — Day 4
1. Broccoli: $\frac{2}{4}$ or $\frac{1}{2}$
   Chicken: $\frac{2}{4}$ or $\frac{1}{2}$
2. Fish: $\frac{2}{5}$
   Chips: $\frac{3}{5}$
3. Bread: $\frac{4}{6}$ or $\frac{2}{3}$
   Cheese: $\frac{2}{6}$ or $\frac{1}{3}$
4. Apple: $\frac{5}{6}$
   Banana: $\frac{1}{6}$
5. Burger: $\frac{4}{7}$
   Ketchup: $\frac{3}{7}$
6. Carrot: $\frac{3}{8}$
   Pizza: $\frac{5}{8}$

Week 12 — Day 5
1. Abu
2. Zack
3. Fred
4. Bai
5. Jay
6. Tom